the making
of a governor

THE MOORE-PREYER-LAKE PRIMARIES OF 1964

the making of a governor

BY JAMES R. SPENCE

JOHN F. BLAIR, *Publisher*
Winston-Salem, N. C.

Copyright © 1968 by JOHN F. BLAIR, *Publisher*
Library of Congress Catalog Card Number 68–25854
Printed in the United States of America
by HERITAGE PRINTERS, INC.
Charlotte, North Carolina

contents

introduction

AN IMPORTANT DAY

SATURDAY, MAY 23, 1964, Yadkinville, North Carolina. To Judge Dan K. Moore, candidate for governor, an important time, an important place.

The candidate will not be rushed. Though supporters have been gathered at the new modern courthouse for some time, he does not arrive until 11:00 A.M. There was a rally at Charlotte last night which lasted until a late hour. Some of his advisers have told him that above all he should get his rest and care for his health. Instead of taking the tiring automobile ride, he has flown up from Charlotte. His car, which is being driven today by Glenn Bass, the professional football player, is air-conditioned, another instrument in cutting down on the candidate's fatigue on a hot day.

The Judge looks good this morning as he steps from his Oldsmobile at the courthouse door with Mrs. Moore. He is six feet, much taller than he has appeared on television, and is down to a slender 170 pounds. He is neat and crisp in his lightweight gray-blue suit, a handsome man by anyone's standards. He smiles as he moves forward to greet his supporters.

Mrs. Moore is tastefully dressed in a yellow outfit that has a wonderfully fresh look on this spring day. She is a woman of great poise, her dignity softened by a natural friendliness. Her hair is swept back and gathered in a manner reminiscent of half a generation ago. It adds to your feeling that this woman would make a First Lady of great bearing.

There are only twenty-five or thirty people who have gathered to see the candidate. Most are inside the lobby of the courthouse. "Babe" Shore, the six-foot-five county Democratic chairman, his wife, and four or five others rush out to greet the Judge. There are no brass bands, no horns, and no fanfare. The Judge moves forward slowly. His athletic frame gives the appearance of one who could challenge any present to a foot race, but he is not in a hurry.

Inside the courthouse, Shore introduces him to all those present, one by one. There are no speeches. Since there is nothing left to do at this immediate spot, the Judge begins to move through the courthouse, meeting the workers in various offices. A bystander remarks that most of the people here are Republicans and cannot vote in the Democratic primary, but he talks to all of them.

Back in the lobby the small crowd has dispersed. Only six people are left, including three reporters.

It is now 11:50. The Judge and his guide leave the courthouse square and visit the Bank of Yadkinville. Seven minutes later they are entering Long & Wishon, a store that sells groceries, seeds, and feeds. At 12:00 they go into Howard Logan's dry goods store; a few minutes later they visit the corner Shell service station. Meanwhile Mrs. Moore and Mrs. Shore sit patiently inside the courthouse.

At 12:40 the Moores, with a half-dozen supporters and three reporters, gather at Red Williamson's restaurant at the edge of Yadkinville for lunch. It is a quiet, relaxed meal. Only the reporters seem restless. Everyone seems happy and encouraged about the campaign. Shore says he believes that the Judge can win on the first primary. His companion believes that it will take two.

By 1:15 the group has formed a small auto caravan and has headed toward the Forbush Volunteer Fire Department. On the way the candidate has his driver turn off the road and drive to the back door of Mrs. Avalon Hall, widow of a former Superior Court solicitor of the district. It is explained that Judge Moore frequently stayed at the Hall home when he held court in Yadkinville.

At 1:30 he turns off the highway again at the home of another old friend, but by 1:35 he is at the Forbush Fire Station shaking hands with the ten men who have gathered there. He makes a short informal talk on vocational education, reducing pupil load, and highways. Back on the road a reporter vents his feelings: "Do you realize that that was the first speech the man has made to a small group in two weeks? I don't think he expects to win. He's not even working for it. How many people has he seen today? Forty? Fifty? It's after two o'clock. The day is more than half over. I'll bet that at least a third of the people he *has* seen today are Republicans. I don't think he's got a prayer. I think he's just going through the motions."

The caravan moves on to the East Bend Community Volunteer Fire Department. This time there are twenty-five or thirty people waiting. They go inside and sit down. This time the speech is a little more formal. The candidate says that he is in favor of protecting the REA, but that there is a place in the state for private power too—that he will seek to reconcile their differences. He says that he has no objection to raising the minimum wage if it can be done without putting a lot of people out of work. A man in the back asks what he thinks of "Sanford." He says that he thinks the Sanford administration has done a lot of good but that "it has been too political."

At 2:55 he is at the Fall Creek Community Volunteer Fire Department. He makes no speech to the forty people gathered there. Shore invites them to the rally at North Wilkesboro tonight. At 3:20 he greets twenty people at the Boonville City Hall, and at 4:00 he is at the Jonesville Fire Department. It is sprinkling rain now. The Judge greets those out front, then goes across the street to a supermarket. He returns shortly with four package boys in white uniforms. At 4:20 Shore calls the crowd inside. There are exactly thirty-six people present. Shore tells them that he used to be a salesman, but that Dan Moore is the best product he has ever had to sell to the people of North Carolina. Moore follows him with his best speech of the day. It almost seems that he is warming up as he progresses.

There is another characteristic of the candidate that now becomes apparent after a day of traveling with him. When he greets people, he centers his entire attention on them and takes ample time with them. No hasty handshakes. No looking over the shoulder to the next man in line.

At 4:54 he turns in at the Community Building next to the West Yadkin Baptist Church. Sixteen people are waiting. They drink Coca-Colas together and talk. Leaning up against a red vending machine, he converses in private tones with four men about the road bond issue. "If that crowd gets in and has this big bond issue, they'll become so powerful that we'll never get them out," he says earnestly. He is talking about the Preyer forces. He continues his personal conversations until 5:10, then goes to his car, where Glenn Bass is waiting, and drives off toward North Wilkesboro.

The day of barnstorming is over, but now he must face the night. The biggest and noisiest political rallies are always at night. After a brief rest at the motel, he will have to meet the huge crowd in the National Guard Armory. They have not seen him and they will expect him to be as fresh as any television performer. They will expect an interesting evening and he will give it to them. He will take off his gloves. He will say that his opponent Dr. I. Beverly Lake is an extreme right-winger and that his opponent L. Richardson Preyer is the candidate of the NAACP and CORE.

An important day? A day like any other day in the campaign. A deceptively slow-paced day. One of the necessary days that Dan K. Moore must live through between his announcement at the last of August, 1963, and election day, November, 1964.

THE "OLD GUARD"
FINDS A NEW LEADER

IN NAPOLEON'S ARMY the "Old Guard" was a body of the emperor's finest, most experienced fighting men. In North Carolina politics the "Old Guard" is the name given the conservative and middle-of-the-road faction that followed Charles M. Johnson to defeat in his battle for the governorship against W. Kerr Scott in 1948. (Its roots go back even further, depending upon which historian is tracing them.) It is the same faction that came back strong in 1952 and won with William B. Umstead. At Umstead's untimely death, there was a period of uncertainty, because Umstead and Luther Hodges had not been close. Many in the Umstead circle viewed the Lieutenant Governor with disdain. Some of the "Old Guard" had not bothered to find out much about the political philosophy of the former vice-president of Marshall Field and Company, who had won the office of lieutenant governor by personal salesmanship without stirring up many real issues. But it soon became clear that, although Hodges was a strong man, he was one of their own.

In 1960, the faction in power could not settle on a leader. First there were trial balloons for Addison Hewlett of Wilmington, Speaker of the House. At one time Hewlett thought that he had the backing of the "Old Guard," but as time went on they moved to another candidate, and he switched to an unsuccessful race for a seat in the U.S. Senate. Then there was John Larkins of Trenton, long-time member of the legislature and state chairman of the Democratic party. Larkins had sometimes crossed Hodges, but he had assets that made him an attractive candidate. Many around the state were saying that he had worked harder for the party than any other living person; that he had earned the governorship. He was particularly strong among the Johnson-Umstead followers. For a time the group close to Hodges toyed with the idea of going along with Larkins, but in the spring (1960) they decided against it.

Dr. I. Beverly Lake was talking of running, but he was unacceptable to the "Old Guard." Although he was a conservative, he was considered a maverick. He had worked on Hodges' "Pearsall Plan," which was designed to fight integration by means of pupil assignment, but had finally devised his own plan, a more conservative plan. Furthermore, he had in some respects become a critic of the Hodges administration.

Attorney General Malcolm B. Seawell was another possible candidate. He had not been clearly identified politically (having been in office only since his appointment by Hodges on April 18, 1958), but Seawell had a knack for getting favorable publicity, and he had received a great deal of it during the Henderson cotton mill strike in the spring of 1959. Labor leader Boyd Payton had claimed that someone in a passing car had thrown rocks through his automobile windshield. Seawell made an investigation and called Payton's story a hoax. The two men then engaged in a continuing newspaper feud until Payton was convicted at the July 13 term of Vance County Superior Court of conspiring to dynamite the boiler room of the Harriett Cotton Mill.

Seawell, on occasion, was a speaker who could not be surpassed. He was young but had the right amount of gray in his hair. He was handsome, slender, and vigorous. He had a good record as a solicitor and as a judge of the superior court. But he did not have financial resources. After much consideration he decided that he could not make the race for the governorship.

Seawell was a personal friend of Terry Sanford. They had shared their private ambitions during the long years of coming up through the ranks. It was understood between them (or so

Sanford thought) that Seawell wanted to be on the North Carolina Supreme Court, as his father had been, and that Sanford wanted to be governor. Sanford kept in close touch with Seawell in late 1959 and early 1960. He was not on very close terms with the Hodges administration and considered Seawell to be his liaison man with the governor's office. Later in the spring, after Seawell had decided not to run, he told Sanford that he would not make the race. He did not know at that time of the forces that were conspiring to get him to change his mind.

Within a matter of days, a group of business and political leaders closely identified with Governor Hodges approached Seawell about running. They pointed to the Lake threat and the Sanford threat. They did not feel that Larkins could win and were not sure that they wanted him to win. They needed a man who was on their team and they had the money to back him. Seawell pointed out that he had a family to consider and that it might not be prudent for him to give up the post of attorney general to grab for the governorship. His persuaders assured him that he would not be left destitute if he lost. Under these circumstances, Seawell became a candidate, less than a week after he had told Sanford that he would not run.

The Seawell candidacy split the "Old Guard." Seawell got 101,148 votes and Larkins got 100,757. Their combined total was more than the 181,692 received by Dr. Lake, but less than Sanford's 269,463.

Faced with this situation, the Hodges-Seawell forces joined Sanford to keep Lake out of the governorship. They gained political advantage by their action, as evidenced by Sanford's role in getting Hodges appointed Secretary of Commerce under President Kennedy. Curiously, Charles M. Johnson, leader of the "Old Guard" in 1948, became a Sanford supporter at the beginning of 1960 because of personal friendship.

Sanford was kind to the business community and to the conservatives. He had marks of the conservative himself. He believed in the movement toward industrialization in North Carolina, and he knew that this took big money—conservative money. He had a large number of wealthy businessmen in his camp. He had found, as all North Carolina governors had found, that it took conservative money to run a gubernatorial campaign. While he was a progressive on the Negro question, he was an easterner with segregation deep within. He had been a strong supporter of the Pearsall Plan.*

In spite of these conservative aspects of Sanford, the "Old Guard" felt left out. Sanford brought into his office Hugh Cannon, Tom Lambeth, and Graham Jones, all men under thirty years of age. The conservatives were accustomed to older men. Sanford appointed Paul Thompson of Fayetteville as National Committeeman, quickly followed by Bill Staton of Sanford in the same post.† He installed Bert Bennett, Jr., his campaign manager, as chairman of the Democratic party, and Hargrove (Skipper) Bowles, Jr., of Greensboro as head of Conservation and Development. None of the men named above were very "liberal." In the older group, Bowles, Bennett, and Thompson were all owners of large businesses which needed a climate that could best be provided by a middle-of-the-road state government. Bowles had once left the Democrats to become an ardent Eisenhower supporter. But these facts were not enough to satisfy the "Old Guard." The Sanford appointees tended to be clannish, were proud of having helped win the governorship,

---

* In certain northeastern counties, the Pearsall Plan was considered too liberal. In those areas Sanford men learned to wink and say, "Don't worry, Old Terry's all right on the Negro question."

† Apparently Thompson wanted the prestige but not the job. He soon resigned in order that Sanford might appoint Staton, but remained a Sanford intimate.

and were not disposed to let bygones be bygones. The "outs" did not like the feel of it.

Many began to turn for new leadership to the able Cloyd Philpott, the new Lieutenant Governor. Philpott was a Piedmont furniture manufacturer who was identified closely with Hodges. He had unquestioned ability, and his next goal in life was to be governor. Then, without warning, death struck him down.

There were other conservatives in the state who could have assumed leadership. There was Woodrow Jones, former state chairman of the Democratic party; Basil Whitener, congressman from the 10th district; and Mel Broughton, former Highway Commission chairman under Hodges (and son of the late Governor Broughton). Dr. Henry Jordan, a former Kerr Scott Highway Commission chairman, wanted to run for governor as a middle-of-the-roader now, with the support of his brother, U.S. Senator B. Everette Jordan, definitely an "Old Guarder." There was Joseph M. Hunt, Jr., former House Speaker. There was Paul Kitchen, former congressman, and there was Dan K. Moore, former superior court judge.

After Philpott's death, the remainder of 1961 and half of 1962 passed with no one making a move to assume leadership of the conservatives. At that point, it was Hunt who moved. He instigated a meeting at Statesville which was attended by Lake, Kitchen, Jones, Moore, and himself. Dr. Henry Jordan was invited to the meeting but could not attend. The inclusion of Lake in such a meeting may surprise some political observers, but his presence was considered so important that he was included as an original planner of the caucus and extended invitations to some of the others.

The question before the meeting was who would lead the conservatives as a candidate for governor in 1964. The five men met with the consciousness that they might be deciding the fate of North Carolina for many years to come. Some were old friends who had great affection for each other, but they knew that their gubernatorial aspirations might collide. Some had already decided that they did not really want the governorship badly enough to make a hard-fought race.

Hunt had hoped to achieve two things in the meeting: (1) to learn who really wanted to make the race, and (2) to find out if all were willing to yield to one leader on whom they might agree. The objectives were partially met in that it became apparent that Kitchen, Jones, and Hunt were willing to count themselves out of the running if one of the others would make the race. In other respects the meeting was somewhat inconclusive.

In 1963, the same group attended the Jefferson-Jackson Day Dinner in Raleigh. They stayed overnight and met together on the following day. This time Dr. Henry Jordan met with them. Again, no one committed himself to the race. All seemed anxious that one step out and take the lead. Some of those present remember that, at one point in the meeting, all agreed that they would support any man in the group who would volunteer to run. All except one. Dr. Lake was not willing to make a commitment that was so all-conclusive.

In spite of the tone of this meeting, it was known that three of those present were making more preparations than the others for a possible run. These three were Lake, Jordan, and Moore.

For years, Dan K. Moore had wanted to run for governor. The year 1964 was very important to him. Now past his middle fifties, he could not wait four or eight years. It was now or never. In early 1963 he began to voice his ambitions to his closest friends. Could he get enough support to run for governor?

His credentials were good. He had come from a good family

background. Five generations back, his ancestor, Captain William Moore, had become the first white settler west of the Blue Ridge Mountains. He was from a long line of lawyers and judges. There had been Charles Moore and Walter Moore, both superior court judges. His own father, Fred Moore, had become a superior court judge at age twenty-eight.

But there was poverty and hard work in Dan Moore's background too. When he was two years of age, his father died. His widowed mother moved to Sylva. They were so poor that young Dan had to perform janitorial duties during high school to help meet expenses.* He earned his expenses at the University of North Carolina, where he made Phi Beta Kappa. He completed law school in one year and began law practice in 1928 in his home town of Sylva.

He built a solid record as a young lawyer, successively becoming town attorney, county attorney, attorney for the board of education, and finally winning a seat in the state legislature in 1941.

He added to his political credentials by enlisting in the Army in 1943, although he was thirty-seven years old. When he returned, he ran for superior court solicitor and won. In 1947, Governor Gregg Cherry appointed him a superior court judge, making him the fourth in his family to hold that position. Ten years later, at age fifty-two, he declined to run for judge again and accepted a position as chief counsel for the Carolinas Division of Champion Papers, Inc.

Not only did Dan K. Moore have a good record on paper; those who knew him could testify that he had been a solicitor and judge of high caliber. He had developed an excellent

---

* Moore's advertising men exploited this poverty-filled childhood during the campaign, which prompted Richardson Preyer to refer to him on one occasion as the "barefoot boy of Champion Paper Co."

reputation in the mountain and piedmont counties in which he had served. This reputation, however, was largely among lawyers. Outside his own district, where he had run for solicitor and judge, he was unknown to the rank and file voters of North Carolina. Although he had served on the State Executive Committee of the Democratic party for many years, Judge Moore was not known to the several hundred Democrats who faithfully attend party gatherings several times each year.

The fact that Judge Moore was a political unknown had its assets. It meant that he could run without being identified immediately with one faction. He had no political scars. He could formulate his own program and pronounce his own feelings on any given issue.

In that spring of 1963, however, he was under no misapprehensions about where his support would come from. He would get no help from the Sanford administration. He needed to unify the forces that had supported John Larkins and Malcolm Seawell four years before, and he needed to attract Lake supporters, if he was to win.

He had heard of the strong support that Dr. Henry Jordan had in many counties of the state. He was aware not only that Jordan was an attractive middle-of-the-roader but also that he had connections with the old Kerr Scott forces which would bring him support from some in the Sanford camp. He was also aware of the forces that were pressing Dr. Lake toward another candidacy. He knew that, if he did not make a move to put himself in a position of leadership, his key friends would end up supporting Jordan or Lake. Therefore he began an intensive effort to line up the kind of support that he felt was necessary before he could decide to run.

His reception was good. There were many moderates and conservatives who could not support Lake and were still looking for a leader. Some who liked Dr. Jordan felt that his age (sixty-five) was against him. One thing was clear: the "outs" wanted "in," and they were anxious to find the most capable man to help them win power again.

By the last of August, 1963, Moore felt that he was ready to make his move. He got in touch with all members of the group who had met in Statesville in 1962 and in Raleigh in 1963 and told them that he felt he had enough support to make the race and that he planned to announce. He went to Raleigh personally to talk to Dr. Lake. He attempted to persuade Lake not to run, but by then pressures had mounted to such an extent that Lake could not very well take himself out of the race. Furthermore, Lake felt that, with the outbreak of the Negro "revolution," he would have a better chance to win than the politically unknown Moore.

Faced with this situation, Moore decided to announce his candidacy almost immediately and thus bulldoze his way into the leadership of the conservatives. There was also the hope, although a slight one, that the Sanford forces would be unable to find a suitable candidate. There were rumors to the effect that Bert Bennett, Jr., at that time the leading Sanford prospect, was finding less than enough support across the state for his candidacy. Since no one else had been groomed to lead the liberals, there was a possibility that Moore, as a middle-of-the-roader, could get Sanford support, particularly if it became a Lake-Moore contest.

Under these circumstances, Judge Moore announced his candidacy on Friday, August 30, just as William D. Caffrey of Greensboro was mounting the petition campaign that would attract L. Richardson Preyer into the race. During the weekend, Dr. Henry Jordan, from a hospital bed in Greensboro, announced that he would not run and that he would support Judge Moore.

section two

THE SANFORD FORCES

IN THE SUMMER OF 1960, after Terry Sanford had been nominated for governor by the Democrats, a supporter went to see him about a possible appointment for a third person.

"Is he the type of man that we can count on four years from now?" asked Sanford.

"Where are we going four years from now, Terry?" inquired the visitor.

Sanford sighed and dropped to a conversational level of extreme frankness. "To tell you the truth," he answered, "I have no idea."

Even though he had no idea what he would want to do in 1964, Sanford, like all men who reach the governorship, wanted to build a loyal following that he could lead, if he chose, at some future time.

In the summer of 1960 there was certainly no "machine."* During the two hard primaries, he and his campaign manager, Bert Bennett, Jr., had selected a county manager in each of the hundred counties, but these were merely citizens who had to work as hard for votes as anyone. They were not political bosses who could command votes. In the fall election against Republican Robert Gavin, after Sanford had backed John F. Kennedy at the Los Angeles convention, they would learn just how hard it would be to muster a majority. The main asset of the Sanford group was that they had made a considerable number of friends in each county. Their second greatest asset was that their man in the governor's chair could make appointments.

There were more than three hundred appointments to be made. While these included some good positions such as that of Commissioner of Revenue and those on the superior court

* In the 1964 campaign, Sanford said, " 'Machine' is what you call the other man's political organization."

(as vacancies occurred), the Utilities Commission, and the Highway Commission, about two hundred were minor indeed. This latter group included a conglomeration of non-paying jobs, memberships on boards, commissions, and committees. While a few of these appointments were sought after, most were of such little importance that they were viewed merely as pats-on-the-back from the governor. They did not constitute such gracious benevolence on the part of the chief executive that he could later ask for political support of the appointees and expect to obtain it. At best, they were poor pay for past favors.

Moreover, even when Governor Sanford made important appointments, he did so with a full realization of the fact that the appointee might oppose him later. He never extracted promises of future support. For example, he appointed Lewis R. (Snow) Holding to the North Carolina Banking Commission. Holding then supported Dan K. Moore in 1964.

Therefore, the question arises, did Sanford and Bennett have a political "machine" in 1963 and 1964? Perhaps the best answer is provided by the results of the 1964 primaries. A "machine" is a "machine" only if it can deliver votes.

However, there was a Sanford faction in North Carolina, as distinguished from the Lake faction and from the "Old Guard," and that faction wanted to keep a friend in the governor's chair. At the end of the 1960 campaigns many Sanford workers recognized that their most dynamic leader was Bert Bennett, Jr. Few had ever heard of him before Sanford selected him to manage his campaign, but now they had seen him in action and knew his ability. A few mentioned that he would be a powerful candidate for governor, but they were realists enough to understand that much could happen before 1964. They were satisfied to see Bennett become state chairman of the Democratic party. In the few quiet moments during which he could think of such things, Sanford himself looked over the field of his friends and saw Bert Bennett as his most likely successor. Lieutenant Governor Cloyd Philpott, with his eyes on the governorship, recognized Bennett as his most likely rival.

After Philpott's death, the field seemed to be wide open for Bennett. It appeared that the "Old Guard" might be the faction without a candidate. But there were several factors conspiring against the possible Bennett candidacy. The foremost of these factors, one that still may surprise North Carolinians, was the fact that Bert Bennett had no real ambition to be governor. Sanford had wanted the governorship very much. Lake wanted the governorship. But Bennett really did not want it. He enjoyed being county chairman in Forsyth County. He enjoyed being Sanford's campaign manager, and he enjoyed being state chairman of the Democratic party. He had no desire to be a candidate, to be the man in the posters, the man in the spotlight.

But what does a man do when he wants his political faction to stay in power, and he is the most qualified leader? He goes along with the idea of remaining the leader (if he is a Bert Bennett), rather hoping that new leadership will arise.

The second factor that conspired against Bennett was completely outside his control. President Kennedy's promotion of Negro "civil rights" had made the President very unpopular in North Carolina. Bennett and Sanford were closely identified with Kennedy. Governor Sanford had generated some unpopularity of his own, and this unpopularity had rubbed off on Bennett. Therefore, in the spring of 1963, Bennett's name was not a vote-getter in North Carolina.

As the Negro "revolution" of 1963 gained momentum,

Bennett became more and more convinced that it would not be wise for him to make the race for governor. However, the question remained, if not Bennett, then who? The name of Robert W. Scott was mentioned, but little interest seemed to be in evidence at that time for the thirty-four-year-old State Grange Master, even though his father's name (that of the late Senator and Governor W. Kerr Scott) was sure to bring votes. And Judge L. Richardson Preyer was mentioned.

Lunsford Richardson Preyer was born January 11, 1919, in Greensboro. His father was William Y. Preyer, destined to become president of the Vick Chemical Company. His mother, May Norris Richardson Preyer, was the daughter of Lunsford Richardson, founder of the Vick Chemical Company. Young Preyer was, of course, named for his maternal grandfather.

Richardson Preyer went to public schools in Greensboro until he was thirteen. At that time his family moved to New York because his father's services were needed there in Vick Chemical. The Preyers did not like New York, however, and returned to Greensboro after two years. Richardson entered Princeton in 1937 and graduated in 1941. Soon thereafter he entered the Navy. He served two years as a torpedo officer on a destroyer in the Atlantic, then was transferred to another destroyer for a second two-year tour in the South Pacific. He was Executive Officer of the destroyer U.S.S. "Preston." His ship was in the thick of the Battle of Okinawa. All the destroyers in Preyer's squadron were sunk except the "Preston" and one other. He was awarded the Bronze Star for bravery in action connected with an assault by Japanese suicide planes.

Preyer entered the Harvard Law School in 1946 and graduated in 1949. In 1950 he returned to his home town of Greensboro and began law practice. Within two years he was appointed judge pro tempore of the Greensboro Municipal

Court, and on July 1, 1956, he was appointed superior court judge by Governor Luther Hodges.

In 1960, when Malcolm B. Seawell resigned as Attorney General to run for governor and Wade Bruton was appointed in his place, friends urged Preyer to run for that office as a steppingstone toward the gubernatorial race in 1964. Preyer weighed the matter carefully and declined. He did not want to move his family to Raleigh at that time, and he felt that the race situation in North Carolina would make the attorney generalship a "hot spot" for the following four years.

After the 1960 campaigns were over, friends talked to Preyer again about the governorship. He admitted that he would be interested if the right situation developed and agreed to begin attending more political meetings around the state so that he would be better known to the professional politicans. At that time he had no way of foreseeing that he would be a federal judge in a matter of months. In early 1961 (also before the federal judgeship matter arose), it appeared that Bennett, Philpott, and others would dominate the field in 1964. At that time a friend wrote to Preyer telling him not to be discouraged by the situation. He recalled for Preyer the Lindberg story, how so many flyers seemed to be ahead of the man who would later be called the Lone Eagle, but how he had worked and prepared almost as if he had no competitors. Preyer wrote back saying that he was no Lindberg but that he would continue to make his preparations.

In 1961, there were three federal judgeships to be filled in North Carolina because of new legislation passed by Congress. It was quickly learned that the two U.S. senators, Sam J. Ervin and B. Everette Jordan (the usual dispensers of federal patronage) favored Superior Court Judge Braxton Craven for the new post in the Western District, defeated gubernatorial candidate Malcolm B. Seawell for the Middle District post, and defeated gubernatorial candidate John Larkins for the Eastern District judgeship. The Craven and Larkins appointments had clear sailing, but the Seawell proposal quickly ran into difficulties. Seawell had lived all his adult life in Lumberton, clearly in the Eastern District, but moved to Chapel Hill as soon as he learned that there was a possibility of his appointment. A group of lawyers in the Middle District rebelled against the idea of appointing Seawell, who was not one of their own, and proposed instead Judge L. Richardson Preyer. Governor Sanford was more friendly toward the latter candidate. He felt that he had paid the Hodges-Seawell forces for their support in the second primary of 1960 by getting Hodges appointed Secretary of Commerce. He had strong friends among the lawyers who did not want Seawell, and Preyer had been a strong Sanford supporter. Therefore it came to pass that President Kennedy, who owed a great deal to Governor Sanford for his early support, did not choose to pick Seawell. (This incident did not improve relations between Governor Sanford and Senators Ervin and Jordan.)

With Preyer in a lifetime judgeship which carried great prestige and a salary of $22,500 per year, few suspected that he harbored gubernatorial ambitions. Indeed, it may be that such ambitions were tossed aside for a time. However, friends had mentioned to Preyer more than once that he would make an excellent governor, and he had not forgotten.

Richardson Preyer had never communicated his gubernatorial ambitions to Governor Sanford or to Bert Bennett during all of this period. When Preyer's name began to be mentioned for the governorship in the summer of 1963, it was not because the Sanford group had spread it. With other citizens, they listened with interest to this new name because they were facing facts as to the Bennett candidacy.

Their attitude was exemplified by that of William Staton of

Sanford, Democratic National Committeeman, in a conversation with a visitor to his office during the second week of August, 1963. He was frank about the problems that Bennett faced and admitted that Preyer interested him if Bennett decided not to run. He also said, "When you sit in my chair, as Democratic National Committeeman, you have to be interested in the whole Party, not in just one or two men."*

On August 22 the *Charlotte Observer* predicted that Bennett would not run for governor, but on August 28 Bennett resigned as state chairman of the Democratic party and began a tour of the state to sound out political opinion.

During the third week of August a personal friend talked to Judge Preyer about the governorship. After much persuasion, Preyer finally said that, if he had an indication of good support from the people of Guilford County, he would be inclined to run. The friend went away somewhat discouraged but mentioned the conversation to William D. Caffrey, Greensboro attorney. Caffrey went into action. Within a short time he made contact with several of his friends in the "Sanford" group and with Bennett himself. Caffrey told them that he planned a campaign to get petitions signed asking Preyer to run. Bennett approved.

Caffrey quickly recruited volunteer women workers in Greensboro and supplied them with petitions. On August 29, the day after Bennett resigned as Democratic Party Chairman, Caffrey ran an advertisement in Guilford County newspapers entitled "An Open Letter to Judge L. Richardson Preyer." The advertisement urged Preyer to run for governor and urged citizens to write in, asking Preyer to run.† By the end of the

* He was also concerned about the selection of a new party chairman to succeed Bennett, one who would be acceptable to all factions. That man turned out to be State Senator Lunsford Crew.

† The next day, August 30, Dan K. Moore announced his candidacy.

Labor Day weekend, more than sixteen thousand people had flocked to sign the petitions. Preyer was very well known and was very popular in Guilford County. The petition campaign was so successful that it made news across the state and introduced many people to a new name in state-wide politics. The petitions put Preyer in a position to be accepted by the Sanford forces, if he chose to run. (If the petition campaign had not been successful, the search for a candidate would have gone on, and Bennett might very well have tackled the job himself.) Preyer quickly conferred with close friends and political advisers and established contact with a number of prominent people in the Sanford camp.

It was decided that Preyer should have an opportunity to meet with many of these leaders before announcing his final decision, and conversely that many of them should have an opportunity to meet with him. Accordingly, a meeting was arranged at the Holiday Inn South in Greensboro on the night of September 8. Some fifty people attended from all sections of the state. They included such leaders as Clifton Benson of Raleigh, Hargrove Bowles, Jr., of Greensboro, Clint Newton of Shelby, Bruce Elmore of Buncombe County, Bruce Poole of Raleigh, and Henry Hall Wilson of Monroe.* Governor Sanford stopped by the meeting for a few minutes.

The next day, Preyer announced that he would be a candidate.

---

* Although Wilson was interested in the Preyer campaign, since he had been a leader in the Sanford group, he remained in his post as a White House aide in Washington and did not participate in the North Carolina primaries.

section three

THE FACTION THAT
HAD A CANDIDATE

DR. I. BEVERLY LAKE first began to think of running for governor in the summer of 1955. He was thrust into prominence by a speech he made on July 12, 1955, to the Asheboro Lions Club. In the speech he advocated that all communities in the state charter nonprofit charitable corporations to operate private schools. These were to be used in the event that Negroes forced integration of the schools. He said in the speech, "We shall fight the NAACP county by county, city by city, and if need be, classroom by classroom to preserve our public schools as long as possible while organizing and establishing other methods of educating our children."

At the time of Lake's statement, Governor Hodges had a committee headed by Rocky Mount businessman Tom Pearsall working on the school integration problem. Lake was an assistant attorney general who was working on that committee in drafting legislation to meet the problem. Hodges was angered by the Lake statement and immediately told newsmen that Lake spoke only as a private citizen. He said that the Lake plan assumed the abandonment of the public school system. Almost immediately after the Hodges statement, the NAACP demanded that Lake be fired. Hodges, who knew that he would run for governor in 1956, could not let himself be caught on the same side of a question as the NAACP. He therefore defended Lake and said that, instead of firing him, he would do his best to retain him. Nevertheless, Lake resigned a few weeks later, and by the end of August he admitted publicly that he had been asked by friends to run for governor. He did not make the race against Hodges in 1956, but the bug had bitten him and would dominate almost a decade of his life.

Lake's credentials for the governorship were equal to those of any of his opponents in 1960 or 1964. He was born at

Wake Forest August 29, 1906, the son of a college professor there. He graduated from Wake Forest College in 1925, obtained a law degree at Harvard in 1929, later obtaining a master's degree (1940) and a doctorate (1947) at Columbia.

After a short association with a Raleigh law firm, he was a professor at Wake Forest Law School from 1932 to 1951. During this time he wrote an important legal book entitled *North Carolina Practice Methods*, which was published by the West Publishing Company in 1952.

The same year, Dr. Lake left teaching to become an assistant attorney general of North Carolina. One of his main duties in that position was to fight, on the side of the state, any integration suits that were brought by Negro citizens. If he was not already so oriented, the State of North Carolina taught him to be a strong segregationist, indeed demanded that he be such in the position that he held.

In 1954, shortly after the Brown decision in which the U.S. Supreme Court struck down school segregation, visitors to Dr. Lake's office in Raleigh found him highly concerned about the new ruling. He feared bloody rioting all through the South. When a vacancy arose in the position of attorney general, Lake expected to move up, but Hodges bypassed him. In 1955, when Lake resigned to practice law, he became a severe critic of the Hodges administration.

By 1959, Lake was in dead earnest about running for governor but was concerned about the problem of financing a campaign. He was still on friendly terms with Terry Sanford, the young Fayetteville attorney who was in the race (but unannounced). On one occasion during the latter part of the spring of 1963 a personal friend encountered Dr. Lake and told him that he was too involved with the Sanford campaign to consider his (Lake's) candidacy. "Well now," said Lake, "I want you to understand that when you're talking about Terry Sanford you're talking about one of my friends."

During the summer and fall of 1963, Lake was still talking like a candidate and looking for finances. His chief supporters and advisers during this period were two former pupils,* Robert Morgan and Archie Taylor, both of Lillington. They set $50,000 as the minimum amount of money necessary to begin. The money did not come forth, and on February 10, 1960, at a Democratic meeting in Sanford, Lake announced that he would not make the race. Sanford was at the meeting and immediately had kind words for the man who had withdrawn. "You certainly had us scared," he added.

The withdrawal was short-lived. Lake's announcement brought forth support, both personal and financial, that he had not heard from before. Within a matter of weeks he announced that he would run after all.

Lake was a maverick in North Carolina politics. The party regulars were for Larkins, Seawell, and Sanford. Lake had no political experience himself and had no campaign advisers who had state-wide experience. Robert Morgan became his campaign manager.

Morgan had run for office locally a number of times (always winning) and had wide acquaintance in the North Carolina General Assembly, where he served as a senator. Like Lake, however, he was a man of strong convictions, and he had been among the minority of legislators who regularly opposed Governor Hodges.

Operating under these difficulties, the Lake forces were able

* There was one aspect of Lake's campaigns that was unique in the history of North Carolina politics. His former students were the backbone of his organization.

to get campaign managers in only about seventy counties, but what Dr. Lake lacked in organization he made up by having an issue. He was the defender of the Southern system of segregation. He attacked the NAACP on television and in speech after speech across the state. He said that Supreme Court decisions were not the "law of the land." He implied that the token integration of a few schools in North Carolina was a result of the softness of the state's leaders on the question, and pointed to South Carolina and other states where not even token mixing of the races had been allowed.

Lake's campaign was so effective that he got almost as many votes as Larkins and Seawell combined and earned the right to a runoff against front-runner Sanford. He fought a bitter second primary, losing by a vote of 275,000 to 352,000. He had spent about $175,000, much less than his opponent.

Since he was not a party regular, Dr. Lake did not think like a party regular after the primaries were over. There was no great rushing to Sanford to help him beat Robert Gavin, the Republican candidate, in the fall. The bitterness of the second primary made it hard to get the Lake forces to back Sanford. After the Los Angeles convention, when Sanford was receiving wide criticism for his support of John F. Kennedy, a write-in movement for Lake developed. Many Democrats urged Lake to repudiate the movement, and as a result he did make a statement saying that he was not a candidate and had nothing to do with the write-in campaign. Sanford supporters felt that the statement left the door open. Lake felt that he had done all that was required of him under the circumstances.

The matter of Lake's write-in campaign came up for discussion at the next meeting of the Young Democrats in Charlotte. The executive committee passed a resolution condemning the write-in movement and praising Lake for doing the same.

Lake, who was at the rally but not at that particular meeting, was misinformed about the content of the resolution. He thought that it criticized him and that it was to be discussed at the evening rally. He went home hurt and angered, leaving a statement to be read to the gathering by one of his supporters. Since the rally was dominated by Sanford supporters, this did nothing to heal party wounds.

Many leading Lake supporters, such as Zalph Rochelle of High Point, actively campaigned for Gavin in the general election, but there is no way to measure whether a substantial number of Lake voters switched to the Republican candidate. Many political observers noted that Eastern North Carolina provided the Democratic votes that gave Sanford and Kennedy their majorities. Eastern North Carolina was strong Lake territory, and many of his supporters must have stayed with the Democrats.

It was not hard for Dr. Lake to decide to run again in 1964. He could see the mistakes of his former campaigns. He was now better known and could get better financing. He was sure that he could build an organization in all the hundred counties this time.

The Negro "revolution" of 1963 would have thrust Lake into the campaign even if he had not wanted to run. His faction demanded leadership to meet what they considered to be a rising crisis. Lake had founded his faction, and there was no leader to take his place. He made his plans to run, hoping that he could announce on February 1, 1964, but Moore and Preyer announced early and forced him to follow suit. He set up a time and place for his announcement, but the death of President Kennedy caused him to postpone it. Then on Saturday, November 30, 1963, he formally entered the race.

THE EARLY CAMPAIGN

WHEN THE *Charlotte Observer* predicted on August 22, 1963, that Bert Bennett would not be a candidate for governor, it cited three reasons: (1) that President Kennedy's civil rights program had made him unpopular in the state, and that this unpopularity had rubbed off on his friend Governor Terry Sanford and on Sanford's chief lieutenant, Bennett; (2) that Bennett was determined to block Dr. I. Beverly Lake's candidacy; and (3) that Bennett had a strong devotion to the Democratic party—putting the party first and himself second.

This newspaper story stunned many Sanford-Bennett followers across the state. Hundreds of them had already written to Bennett offering their support. Phil Carlton of Pinetops, N.C., only twenty-five years of age but already a veteran of the Sanford campaign, had promised to give Bennett a year of his time and was already renting a suite at the Carolina Hotel in Raleigh (presumably with Bennett's money) as preliminary campaign headquarters. He got in touch with Bennett and asked what was happening. He learned that no decision had been made but that there was some uncertainty about the future.

Charlie H. Smith, who had been named Outstanding Young Democrat in the United States while a student at Western Carolina College, was on the pay roll at the First Union National Bank in Charlotte but had been assigned to work with the Bennett campaign. Like Carlton, he suddenly faced an uncertain future.

Bennett remained silent for six days, then resigned as party chairman and began a tour of the state to talk to his political friends. On the 29th, Guilford County newspapers carried the advertisement urging Federal Judge L. Richardson Preyer to run for governor.

While Bill Caffrey and his friends spent the long Labor Day

weekend collecting coupons from their mailbox and gathering signatures for a petition asking their man to run, the Moore forces sprung two well-timed announcements. The first was from Dr. Henry Jordan, and the second was from Senator Sam J. Ervin, Jr., both offering support in the gubernatorial race. Jordan made his announcement from his hospital bed in Greensboro, where he had been a patient for a week with a gallstone attack. Until that time Jordan had been soliciting support across the state for his own candidacy and was reputed to have a considerable following. Because of his fights in the Senate on civil rights matters, Ervin bore the reputation at that time of being the most popular Democrat in North Carolina.

During the week following Labor Day, political reporters discovered that Judge Moore had been to Raleigh and had met with Dr. Lake during the previous week in an attempt to persuade him not to run for governor. They also reported that Robert W. Scott of Haw River was seriously considering the race. This last bit of intelligence came from the Scott farm on the occasion of a dove shoot which was attended by 125 men, many of whom were more experienced in political wars than in dove wars.

Preyer's announcement on September 9 had been preceded by considerable preparation. There had been wide communication among Sanford supporters. Conferences with Bennett determined that he did not want to make the race (for the exact reasons given in the *Charlotte Observer* story on August 22). His tour of the state had confirmed his opinion that it was not a proper time for him to run. Phil Carlton agreed to stay on and work for Preyer, and at the First Union National Bank, Charlie Smith was assigned to Preyer. Carlton immediately used the WATS line telephone service which he had installed

at the Carolina Hotel to set up a meeting of Sanford forces at
the Holiday Inn South in Greensboro on September 8. The
purpose of the meeting was not to decide on a candidate, as
was later claimed by opponents. That had already been decided. It was to allow long-time political friends to meet the
man whom they would be asked to support. It was considered
a courtesy to have the meeting take place before Preyer's
formal announcement.

Although Bert Bennett did not openly announce his support
of Preyer until September 17, he went to work immediately.
He took from his files the stack of letters that were commit-
ments to his own candidacy and began calling the people involved, asking them to support Preyer instead of himself.
Carlton was on the WATS line with the old list of Terry
Sanford's campaign managers. Except for Preyer's own wide
acquaintance with people throughout the state, the stack of
letters and the old list were the two most important beginning
points in the campaign.

Preyer's actual resignation from the federal bench came on
October 9. The following Saturday he began his personal
campaigning by traveling with two hundred people from
Eastern North Carolina to Washington, D.C., for a weekend
of football. He gained many supporters on this trip, but some
of the Easterners found it hard to communicate with the
scholarly young candidate from the Piedmont. Some pro-
nounced him downright shy and said that he would not make a
good candidate.

On the day that Preyer went to Washington (October 12),
Judge Moore issued an eleven-page statement outlining his
views on a number of political matters. His campaign leaders
later claimed that the newspapers did not adequately report
this statement. While there can always be some question about

what is "adequate," obviously the document could only be summarized in newspaper stories. Among his interesting statements were the following: (1) "The Negro deserves equality of opportunity, but it will not come through violence or civil rights legislation. I do not believe you can legislate equality. It must be earned." (2) "We should have equality of education in all counties, large and small, and necessary book and school fees should be paid by the state."

On October 17, Charlotte television station WBTV attempted to poll the legislators who were assembled in Raleigh in special session. Out of 143 lawmakers they obtained answers from 66. Of these, 39 favored Dan K. Moore for the governorship, 25 favored Richardson Preyer, and 2 favored Dr. I. Beverly Lake. Lake had not announced his candidacy at that time.

On November 5, the *Charlotte News* reported that attorney Allen Bailey of that city would manage Dr. Lake's campaign, and on November 11, Preyer announced that he had selected Raleigh tax attorney N. A. Townsend as his manager. In retrospect, it is significant that, although both men worked hard, neither ever became the top trusted aide of his candidate.

A New Highway Bond Issue?

On November 21, speaking in Raeford, Judge Preyer proposed a new road bond issue for North Carolina. He said that in 1966 the bonds issued by the Kerr Scott administration would be paid off and that the one-cent-per-gallon tax could then be used to pay for a new bond issue. This was the first new idea of the campaign, although a number of people had been giving some consideration to the same plan. On December 14, Judge Moore told a breakfast gathering in Waynesville that North Carolina could have a new highway bond issue without an increase in taxes. He then interjected a new idea of his own, that if surpluses continued, the state might even get a reduction in taxes.*

In the meantime, Dr. Lake, in his opening speech (at Rocky Mount), said that he was for a "steadily proceeding highway construction program" but was opposed to a "wasteful crash program."

LITERACY TESTS FOR VOTING

On December 30, Judge Moore noted that Bert Bennett, Jr., favored abolishing literacy tests for voting, and called attention to the fact that Bennett was a key Preyer supporter. He said that he favored retaining the tests. The next day Preyer announced that he disagreed with his friend Bennett. He said that North Carolina had not abused literacy tests by employing them to deny voting rights to qualified citizens. He said that, instead of abolishing the tests, we should declare war on illiteracy.

This exchange was typical of the campaign. Judge Moore was trying to establish his credentials among voters who were conservative on the race issue. When he brought up the literacy test he did so because of the race question. On the other side, Judge Preyer, in trying to avoid a Moore trap, overstated his case grievously. He had every reason to know that certain counties in North Carolina had used the literacy test to deny voting rights to Negroes. In any case, the subject never became an issue in the campaign.

THE RURAL ELECTRIC COOPERATIVES

On January 4, 1964, Richardson Preyer took a strong stand in favor of maintaining the present role of REA's in North Carolina.

---

* Moore was able to get that reduction at the 1967 General Assembly.

At the time of this statement, Robert Scott was still believed to be considering the possibility of running for governor. If he had come to any conclusion about the matter, he had not informed the public. Scott had been very closely identified with the REA's, and there were reports to the effect that they were ready to support him financially.

When Scott decided not to run, apparently the word got to the Preyer forces before it was announced to the general public. Preyer took his stand with the REA's only three days before Scott announced his decision.

Judge Moore, who was busy lining up the support of the Duke Power Company and the Carolina Power and Light Company, had no word at that time for the REA's. Dr. Lake was also silent on this issue.

THE JUNIUS SCALES CASE

On January 6, Judge Preyer, anticipating criticism from his opponents, discussed with newsmen in Raleigh his role in the case of Junius Scales, convicted Communist of Greensboro.

Preyer said that he and Welch Jordan, another Greensboro attorney, were appointed by the court to defend Scales in 1954. He said that he and Jordan withdrew from the case a short time later because they believed that Scales was going to attempt to use the courtroom as a soapbox to advocate Communism.

Preyer said that, years later, after Scales had been convicted, he was asked to sign a petition in behalf of Scales on a motion to reduce sentence. He said that he declined to sign the petition, but instead wrote a letter to the presiding judge outlining his knowledge of Scales' background.

On January 8, Allen Bailey, Dr. Lake's campaign manager, challenged Preyer's statement that he did not sign the petition. Bailey showed newsmen what he said was a photostatic copy of an official government press release. Preyer's name was one of thirty-five which were typed on a list.

Preyer forces then got in touch with Ed Guthman, a Justice Department official in Washington, who made a statement to the effect that Preyer's name was not on the petition, but was typed on a list by pardon attorney Reed Cozart. The list was attached to the press release announcing the commutation of Scales' prison sentence.

The following day Dr. Lake personally issued a statement saying that Judge Preyer "admits that while on the bench he used the influence of his office to intercede for a man who had been convicted by two North Carolina juries of belonging to an organization which teaches and advocates the overthrow of the government of the United States by force and violence." "It really does not matter," Lake continued, "whether he signed the petition or wrote a letter. I would not have done either."

It is interesting to note that, at the time of Judge Preyer's letter, the *New York Times* ran an editorial saying that it approved of his action because "one political prisoner in America is too many."

"Smoking and Health"

On January 11, the Surgeon General of the United States issued a 387-page report entitled "Smoking and Health," which said, in essence, that smoking was a major health hazard. On January 23, Dr. Lake talked about this problem in a speech to the Edenton Junior Chamber of Commerce. He called for a thorough research program into the smoking-health controversy. He said it serves no purpose to question a federal report linking cigarette smoking with lung cancer unless we are prepared to offer convincing proof that it is inaccurate.

He said that if elected he would urge other tobacco-growing states to participate in a regional research effort. He further stated that he would ask the General Assembly for funds for research at N. C. State to determine and report to all the world exactly what, if any, health hazard is involved in the use of North Carolina tobacco.

OTHER JOUSTING

Dan K. Moore, speaking in Goldsboro on January 13, called Richardson Preyer a "starry-eyed liberal" and said that Dr. Lake offered North Carolina only "retreat."

On January 18, Preyer, speaking to a coffee-and-doughnut gathering of two hundred in Thomasville, promised to see that the town got "a new railroad underpass." He noted that ambulances and emergency vehicles often had to wait for trains two hundred cars long. Judge Moore denounced the promise as "political bribery" and continued to mention the incident throughout the campaign.

On January 23, in a speech to the High Point Rotary Club, Moore brought up two new subjects. He discussed tax concessions to new industry and put himself on record against them, and he discussed the federal government's two-price system for cotton (which caused local textile mills to have to pay 8-1/2 cents more per pound than their foreign competitors), which he also opposed.

THE "SECRET MEETING"

In retrospect, there can be little doubt that January 24 was a turning point in Judge Moore's campaign. On that date he issued a statement accusing L. Richardson Preyer and Sanford administration officials of participating in a "secret" meeting on September 8, 1963, at the Holiday Inn South in Greensboro. He said that administration insiders named Preyer as their candidate at the motel meeting after Bert Bennett, Jr., of Winston-Salem, declined to run. Moore said, "The people of North Carolina have demonstrated time and time again that they do not like for a governor to hand pick his successor. And they certainly do not like for a governor to use the power and prestige of his office to insure the election of the man he has chosen."

"Does Mr. Preyer really expect the people of North Carolina to believe that there is no significance in the fact that he announced his candidacy on September 9, the day after the meeting with the Sanford-Bennett group?" Moore asked.

Preyer immediately issued a statement saying that he was proud of the support of Bert Bennett. He said that there was nothing secret about the meeting at the Holiday Inn, that more than fifty people were present, and that it was one of a number of meetings that he had attended after more than sixteen thousand people in Guilford County had petitioned him to run.

Moore's statement said that among those present at the Holiday Inn meeting were Clifton Benson, State Highway Commissioner, of Raleigh; Bruce Poole, Sanford campaign worker, of Raleigh; Hargrove Bowles, Jr., Chairman, Board of Conservation and Development; Clint Newton, political leader, of Shelby; and Bruce Elmore, political leader, of Buncombe County. He also said that Henry Hall Wilson, former Sanford campaigner and now an aide to President Johnson, came to the meeting "to give his stamp of approval to the chosen candidate."

A Kinston businessman, Felix Harvey, issued a statement saying, "There was nothing secret about it, and it did not pick Preyer. We asked Judge Preyer to come out so that we could size him up. Governor Sanford came by to say that he wasn't going to tell the people who their next governor ought to be. After thanking us for helping him with his programs he left and went to Raleigh."

In High Point the next day, Dr. Lake did not specifically mention the "secret meeting" but said that his Greensboro opponent "is trying hard to keep the people from remembering that he was chosen by the Sanford-Bennett machine." He went on to say that it would be embarrassing for Preyer to remember that he really was the "second choice of the machine." He then referred to Bert Bennett's survey which showed that he probably could not win.

These statements, which both Moore and Lake continued to repeat in various forms throughout the campaign, succeeded in convincing the public that there was something sinister about the Greensboro meeting (which was untrue) and that Preyer's campaign was closely allied to the Sanford administration (which was true). Since Sanford was not enjoying great popularity at that particular time, Preyer's campaign was damaged.

A Four-Lane East-West Highway

Also in his High Point speech, Dr. Lake proposed a four-lane highway from the ports of Wilmington and Morehead to the Tennessee line. Such a highway had been first proposed by Malcolm B. Seawell when he was a candidate for governor in 1960. Like Lake in 1964, he was defeated in the first primary, and North Carolina is still without the highway.

A CAMPAIGN RALLY

THE SCENE is the Greensboro Coliseum; the time, 8:30 A.M., Saturday, January 25, 1964.

The great building is an ocean of empty seats. A temporary stage has been placed near the south end of the floor, which is set up for a basketball game tonight. The fine hardwood floor has been covered with homosote board to protect it during the day's events. Last night there was an ice hockey game in this space. Coliseum manager Bob Kent's men were on duty until midnight to change the facilities. Now they are back on the job setting up and testing microphones, putting up a row of curtains behind the stage, and doing a hundred other last-minute jobs.

The professional decorator arrives and begins to string red-white-and-blue bunting around the stage and auditorium. He has been provided with eight huge photographs of candidate Richardson Preyer. His men begin to mount them on the catwalk around the ceiling. At that distance the photographs look small, but acceptable.

Ted Cramer and Phil Carlton arrive. Cramer is a professional advertising man, who has put together the program for the day and made arrangements for all the professional talent. Carlton is the polished young man in his middle twenties who has headed the state-wide effort to sell tickets at $10.00 each. He is already a veteran of another gubernatorial campaign four years ago. Someone asks him how many people he expects for the rally. He replies that some of his co-workers are counting on 5,000, but that his personal estimate is 4,200. Cramer begins working with the Coliseum men on the sound system.

Someone is worried about the fact that the stage is so far down. If only 5,000 people are coming, the hall may look too empty. Cramer explains that it was necessary to place the stage below the permanently mounted loudspeakers because of feed-back into the microphones. A test reveals that the mike at the speaker's rostrum is effective only from a distance of about two inches. Carlton says that the candidate cannot be expected to work that close. Workers move another microphone into its place and the testing continues.

Charles Kivett arrives. He is an immaculate young man of thirty-six, graying slightly around the temples. He has resigned his position as a bank vice-president to work full time with Richardson Preyer's campaign. He is in charge of the entire rally. He quickly surveys the situation and notices that there is a huge area of the floor at the north end that is empty. He gets assistance from some of the men standing around and begins moving chairs into the space. No additional chairs— just rearranging for effect. The hall must look as crowded as possible.

George Gobel, the television personality who has been billed as the star entertainer for the event, comes to the stage with the small band that has been provided for him and begins working out his music. Soon the word is circulating among those present that Gobel is ill, with a temperature of 102. Several express doubts as to whether he will be able to go on. By 10:15 he has his routine worked out, puts on huge dark glasses and a large hat, turns up his overcoat collar, and eases out the back door into the unseasonable gale wind. Indeed he does appear ill. There is no humor in the face of this comedian.

The high school bands begin arriving: Grimsley, Page, Dudley, and High Point. The main entrance at the rear of the Coliseum is closed because of the high winds. The huge band instruments must pass through a tiny door. Soon there are enough to begin the tuning-up process, which continues.

Kivett is worried about the signs with the names of the

counties. These have been scattered throughout the seating area in the fashion of a national political convention. He notices that some have fallen down and expresses some exasperation with the man who decided not to tie them. He also wants to make sure that there is a sign for each county. Someone goes to count them.

A few people are beginning to arrive now, and some of them are coming in the back entrance. They are supposed to go through the turnstiles at the east entrance, where ticket-takers are stationed. Kivett sends someone to the back door to direct traffic.

Some of the entertainers are coming in. Arthur Smith of Charlotte and his company of performers arrive and get friendly direction to their dressing room. Arthur is the nationally televised celebrity of "Guitar Boogie" fame.

Lula Belle and Scotty Wiseman of Spruce Pine, North Carolina (of National Barn Dance fame in the thirties and recently in demand again), can't find their dressing room. They are rather embarrassed to explain their plight to the doorman. He finds Cramer, who directs them to an area with two additional dressing rooms.

A man brings his little girl to ask the doorman when George Gobel will be back. She wants his autograph and will wait as long as is necessary.

The Dixie Colonels, a barbershop group, arrive, and Doc Watson, the blind folk singer from Deep Gap, North Carolina.

It is eleven o'clock now. In twenty minutes the high school bands will begin to play. The hostesses are pouring in now, mostly young housewives who have left their children with babysitters. They are wearing dresses of either red, white, or blue and hats and ribbons boldly proclaiming "Preyer for Governor." There will be about fifty of them, and they will help direct the people and keep them supplied with hot dogs and drinks. The whole occasion seems to brighten up on their arrival.

They open the turnstiles now, and people begin drifting into the great empty Coliseum. They wander around for a bit, locating their particular county sign, then move off to shake hands with friends they've spotted. Some of the people are bringing their own signs and banners.

Cramer tests the microphones one last time and decides that he has done the best he can. The decorator ties the last of the huge Preyer photographs in place. Now, behind the stage, two huge signs are being raised. They are of the billboard type with a picture of Judge Preyer in a crowd with attorney Bill Caffrey and other admirers close in all around. Two of these make an effective background.

Carlton asks Kivett if he can be provided with one of the walkie-talkies. When Kivett offers one, he realizes that Carlton is kidding him. "I just thought a walkie-talkie would make me look important." The joke is welcome in the rising tension. But the walkie-talkies are no joke. Communication between all those responsible for different phases of the rally will be a problem.

An ambulance and two attendants arrive to be on duty all day, and the Coliseum first-aid room opens—reminders of how many unforeseen things can happen at such an event.

In the corridors outside, the caterers are preparing 20,000 hot dogs and enough coffee and soft drinks to wash them down. They will begin serving at 11:30.

Someone checks the Coliseum parking lot and reports that it is filling up fast. The high school bands begin to play one at a time. They applaud each other, but now there are enough people in their seats to give substantial applause themselves.

The performers are dressed now and wandering around the corridors backstage. Arthur Smith's men are in bright red vests, and Scotty has a red print shirt that matches Lula Belle's dress (which he will later claim she made from a tablecloth), but the outstanding outfits are worn by the singing group, the Dixie Colonels. Their uniforms are yellow, from their wide-brimmed hats to their patent-leather shoes. Their hair is now a becoming gray. One of Arthur's men has left a coat in a motel and asks the doorman to be on the lookout for a taxi that's bringing it. Another finally locates his wife, who is also one of the performers.

Buses are arriving now. Mecklenburg County has sent 500 people. There is a huge group from Alamance. Little Dare County has sent a delegation all the way from Manteo. It is soon apparent that almost all the counties will be represented. Outside and in the outer foyers there is almost a traffic jam as people stop to visit with one another. This situation is complicated by the opening of the concession stands. Hundreds flock to begin eating. There are two tables selling "Preyer for Governor" hats at a dollar each. They can hardly make change rapidly enough.

Then the house lights dim and the spotlights catch a huge flag at the south end of the building. A band plays "The Star Spangled Banner," and the program is under way.

The two masters-of-ceremonies are Bob Poole, the radio personality of Greensboro, and Ty Boyd, the popular television announcer of Charlotte. At the north end of the building listeners note that there is enough volume but that the words of the announcers are not distinct enough to be understood. Technicians are notified and adjustments are attempted.

The Loonis McGlohon Sextet, a jazz group from Charlotte,

lead off on the entertainment. There are some jazz fans in the audience who are appreciative, but many people are going in and out and wandering around to visit various delegations.

Lula Belle and Scotty bring on a bright act of good string music and comedy, but it is hard to get the attention of the full audience.

Nice formica counters have been set up for the press down the east side of the floor, but it turns out that this is just behind the Grimsley High School Band. The reporters can't take the noise. Phil Carlton quickly has the counters moved to the other side of the floor and has food and drinks brought to the newsmen. They seem happy now.

A nice-looking gentleman, a double amputee, is rolled in by wheel chair and placed near the press section. A quick glance reveals that there are several other people in wheel chairs in attendance.

It is now 12:30. The Dixie Colonels and Doc Watson have finished their performances and received good applause. People are still going in and out. But now someone notices that the Coliseum is filling. More are coming in. Anyone can see that more than 5,000 are in their seats. A wave of relief passes over Kivett, Cramer, and Carlton. The event is already a success.

Now Arthur Smith and his group bound onto the stage. Their song is a catchy one:

> I've laid around and stayed around
> This old town too long,
> This old town too long,
> Summer's almost gone . . . .

By this time the audience is clapping in time with the music. Soon feet are stomping and signs are being pounded on the floor, all with the beat of the song. A couple of men are so caught up by the music that they bounce up and start doing a buck and wing, but when the television camera comes around to catch them, they quickly sit down.

The rally is moving now and everyone is grateful to Smith. He swings into "Guitar Boogie," and the house comes down with cheers.

Now they introduce Honey Lucas from Raleigh, a little girl with a bright lilting voice, who has received some fame for doing a new song called "North Carolina." She is pretty, of college age, and can project a song across the footlights. The audience loves her. Then the MC comes back onstage and says, "Ladies and Gentlemen, we now introduce the official campaign song." Honey belts it out:

> Hey, look him over, he's your kind of guy
> Preyer for Gov-nor, on Preyer you can rely . . . .

There is not a sad face in the whole Coliseum. People are laughing, enjoying themselves, and enjoying the entertainment.

Now comes the featured performer, little George Gobel. He borrows Scotty Wiseman's guitar as he goes onstage. He has been nauseated only minutes ago, but now he goes on as if nothing were wrong. After a minute or two onstage he coughs a few times and says that he feels it only fair to tell the audience that he is a victim of his travels—up North one day, down South the next, in and out of air-conditioning. "To tell you the truth," he says, "I've got a hangover." Then he tells a long distasteful tale about backing out of a hot shower into a cold doorknob with a key in it, but finishes up with a delightful audience-pleasing routine about an announcer on a 4:30 A.M. radio program selling everything from patent medicines to funerals. He goes offstage into a mob of autograph seekers and holds a straight unsmiling face for a few signatures. Then he rushes off to be sick again.

Now they introduce the mayor of Greensboro, David Schenck; Oscar Burnett, general chairman of the rally; Nat Townsend, Preyer's state-wide campaign manager; and "Mr. Will" Preyer, father of the candidate. No one has expected "Mr. Will" to say anything, but he does. He is seventy-five years old now but looks no more than sixty. He is the former president of the vast Vick Chemical Company (now Richardson-Merrill) and has been known for years as an excellent speaker in his own right. He doesn't make a political speech, but a personal speech. Some are apprehensive as he begins to tell of his son's early life, and of how he and his wife worried about their son's safety through World War II when the latter was serving on a destroyer in the South Pacific. No one needs to be apprehensive. He keeps well within the bounds of good taste and is highly effective.

Now they cap this performance by bringing on the candidate's wife, vivacious Emily, and the five children. She doesn't make a speech, merely introduces the children, but she brings the house down. Some are already saying that she is the most popular wife of a gubernatorial candidate in North Carolina history.

The house lights dim, and in the northeast corner of the building the spotlight picks out the candidate, Judge L. Richardson Preyer. The crowd cheers and the bands play as he makes his way across the building and down the west side of the basketball court to the stage. He is moving slowly because the crowd is closing in around him. He stops to shake hands with many. Photographers are everywhere, from television and the newspapers. Someone notices that the music is the new campaign song, "Hey, Look Him Over."

The candidate has had a hard week, but now on stage Preyer begins his best speech to date: "Thank you for your hectic and very warm welcome to our secret meeting here this afternoon."

The crowd roars its appreciation.

CAMPAIGN MID-POINT

ON JANUARY 26, the day after the big Preyer rally, Governor Sanford noted recent comments by Lake and Moore about the "Sanford-Bennett machine."

The Governor, a veteran campaigner himself, who in days past had had occasion to talk about another Governor, said he had noticed that the candidates were beginning to call names, "including mine."

"I suppose this is only natural," said the Governor, "but I have something to say about it. I have at least 88 different irons in the fire, programs and projects and things ranging from special schools for dropouts to seafood research." Then he itemized the 88 "irons" one by one.

He concluded his statement by saying, "If the candidates will let me attend to these duties, I will gladly leave the campaigning to them."*

On January 27, Preyer began a state-wide tour of the hundred counties. He started with a handshaking tour in

---

* Those close to the Governor made this assessment of his attitude toward the 1964 primary: Mr. Sanford was experienced enough in North Carolina politics to know that his support would hurt his candidate, but he let his anxiety get the better of him during the second primary and openly endorsed Preyer at the last minute. The following story is of interest in connection with Sanford's endorsement of a primary candidate for governor:

In the first primary of the 1960 campaign, when Sanford was running against John Larkins, I. Beverly Lake, and Malcolm Seawell, he became concerned that many of the old Scott "branch head boys" were being pulled away by Lake and Larkins. He needed something dramatic that would assert his leadership of the old Scott forces. He chose to do this by attacking Governor Hodges, who at that time was quite unpopular in Eastern North Carolina. In a speech at Greenville, he attacked Hodges on the question of his Highway Commission. He said that the commission had become cold-blooded and out of touch with the people, relying more on the point system than on human needs. Sanford later recalled that after that speech he went home and "sweated it out" for twenty-four hours, afraid that Hodges would not say anything. He need not have worried. Hodges fought back in a blistering statement that included an endorsement of Malcolm Seawell. All this showed that Sanford was definitely anti-Hodges, and Sanford moved a step closer to victory.

Macon. In a speech at Andrews he pledged that he would do everything in his power to protect the people from unfair and unreasonable rates and charges for utility services.

The big news in the Preyer camp, however, was the reaction to the rally in Greensboro. Some of the opposition forces were busy circulating a rumor that most of the eight thousand people at the rally were children, but more objective observers agreed that the Preyer forces had scored a huge success. Political columnist William A. Shires described the rally as "something new under North Carolina political sun— a far cry from the old country-style barbecue and brunswick stew suppers and Saturday speechmaking on the court-house lawn."

In Greensboro, Moore's county manager, Herbert Seymour, accused Preyer of using the schools to further his candidacy. He said that school principals used public address systems to notify teachers that free tickets to the Preyer rally were available in the principal's office. Someone asked Seymour if he intended to demand an investigation. He said that he did not because he did not know of any law that had been broken.

On the same day, in Durham, candidate Moore himself declared that his political philosophy is somewhere "between the dangerous extremes represented by my major opponents in this campaign." This was a theme that he would repeat many times during the campaign, a theme that contributed substantially to his victory.

Moore also issued a statement saying that a much larger percentage of the state's secondary road construction should be handled by private contractors. He said that during a fifteen-month period ending December 31, 1962, 70 per cent of the state's secondary road funds were used on projects completed by state forces.

On January 28, while Preyer was campaigning in Swain County, Lake was in New Bern discussing problems of the seafood industry.

A TELEVISION DEBATE?

On January 31, Jesse Helms, vice-president of WRAL-TV in Raleigh, offered free time for televised debates by the candidates. He suggested that there should be one program in February, one in March, two in April, and two in May.

Dan K. Moore and I. Beverly Lake immediately accepted the offer, but L. Richardson Preyer's campaign manager, Nat Townsend, made his acceptance conditional. He suggested that an impartial station originate the program. This apparently referred to WRAL-TV's support of Dr. Lake. Lake's former law partner, A. J. Fletcher of Raleigh, owned a substantial interest in the station.

Helms replied to Townsend that, since any act on his part in connection with the campaign would be suspect, he could only "express the hope that the candidates for governor will now make their own arrangements for joint television appearances."*

On February 5, WRAL-TV withdrew its offer, saying the reason was that one of the candidates had rejected the offer.

Insiders later related some of the problems that were involved in the proposed television debate. Bert Bennett had objected to Preyer's appearing on unfriendly WRAL-TV. He argued that such a debate could be crucial, as in the Kennedy-Nixon campaign, and that bad lighting or bad make-up could ruin a candidate (again citing the case of Nixon). While negotiations for a neutral television station were under way,

---

* This was the beginning of a feud between WRAL-TV and the Preyer forces which would be very costly to the latter.

Dr. Lake became worried that there would not be enough time on the air to discuss the issues properly. But the man who finally stopped the whole idea was Joe Hunt of Greensboro, Moore's representative in the television negotiations. Hunt was convinced that his candidate had nothing to gain by such a debate, but he did not want to announce publicly that his candidate was unwilling to debate. He therefore "filibustered" the negotiations to death.

THE TEN PER CENT PAY RAISE
FOR STATE EMPLOYEES

On Monday, February 3, 1964, Judge Moore announced that he would ask the next General Assembly for an across-the-board pay raise of at least 10 per cent for all state workers.

The next day Judge Preyer called the proposal "fiscal irresponsibility" and said that such a raise would cost $40 million and that the promise was inconsistent with Moore's pledge to hold down spending in state government.

On Thursday, Moore answered Preyer by saying that state workers were the "forgotten people of the Sanford administration"; that it had been seven years since they had had a general pay increase; and that he would pay for the raise out of the state's surplus "with millions of dollars left over." He added that Sanford had given "generous pay raises to many political appointees already earning more than $10,000 per year."

Judge Moore had been advised that the pay increase proposal would be a political master stroke. It was reasoned that it would get literally thousands of votes from state employees, but that it would alienate very few rank-and-file voters across the state. The advice was correct, but there were some uneasy moments about the matter, and Judge Moore felt it necessary to defend his promise time and time again during the remainder of the campaign. It should be added that there were more uneasy moments in the Preyer camp than in Moore's over this issue.

On Friday, Director of Administration Hugh Cannon, a Sanford insider, said that his department had calculated that Moore's proposed pay raise would cost $39,100,000. Then he made a statement that would be argued about at least until the end of the fiscal biennium in 1965: that there would be no large surplus on hand at the end of the biennium. He said that the last legislature had changed the method by which revenue was estimated and that the new method had proved to be highly accurate.

On February 19, Fred Royster, chairman of the State Personnel Council, disputed Moore's claim that state workers had not received a general pay increase in seven years. He said that, after workers received an 11.5 per cent increase and a 3 per cent increase, both in 1957, they received another 3 per cent raise in 1959, a 5 per cent raise in 1961, and a flat $120-per-year raise in 1963. He added that two-thirds of the workers receive a 5 per cent raise every year in the form of a merit increase and that 10,000 workers had been upgraded during the preceding six months.

Judge Moore answered by saying that, within "the past 48 hours," the Sanford administration had given large pay raises to high-salaried employees but nothing to the low-salaried workers.

Also on February 19, Dr. Lake ridiculed Moore's pay-raise proposal in a speech at Tarboro. He said, "To make up the $25 million per year we are now spending over and above our present tax revenue, plus $20 million per year for a ten percent salary increase would require an increase of 25 per-cent in your income tax, or an increase in sales tax from 3 to 4 cents."

In Asheville, on February 25, Judge Moore issued a statement saying that the pay raise would cost only $20 million from the General Fund for the biennium. He said the reason for this was that 40 per cent of state employees work for the Highway Department and would be paid from highway funds. He said that there were many other employees in the same category who were paid out of other self-sustaining funds. This statement was puzzling to political observers because, even if its facts were correct, it did not refute Cannon's claim that the total pay raise would cost $39.1 million. Further, since Judge Moore had said that he was going to pay for the pay increase with the surplus from the General Fund, it raised questions about how the Highway Department and other "self-sustaining funds" would obtain the additional money.

On April 2, Judge Moore again defended his pay raise proposal and said that he expected a surplus of $100 million at the end of the current biennium. His position was supported by a statement on April 6 by State Treasurer Edwin Gill. Gill predicted a "substantial" surplus.

On April 9, Judge Moore issued a statement from Raleigh saying that Judge Preyer and Governor Sanford had sought to imply that he was advocating spending $67 million for a pay raise to state employees. He said that the 10 per cent raise would cost the General Fund only $15 million for the biennium. No mention was made of the previous $20 million estimate contained in the Asheville statement of February 25.

On April 13, State Treasurer Gill gave further support to the Moore position. He said that he estimated a surplus of $75 million to $80 million at the end of the biennium. Since Gill was an old and respected expert on the matter, his word was the final authority. No one argued with him, and everyone proceeded on the assumption that the surplus would be there.

On April 23, in a television interview at High Point, a reporter asked Moore which program he would put first if it turned out that there was not enough money for all the programs he had advocated. Judge Moore said that he was committed to give the 10 per cent pay raise to state employees.

The Preyer forces knew that they were beaten on the issue, but Judge Preyer himself insisted on formulating what he considered to be a fair program for state workers. He announced that program on May 10. It consisted of a new hospital insurance plan, additional longevity pay, and compensation for unused sick leave. He said that the program would cost $5 million per biennium.

Three days later all three candidates appeared at a fish fry for state employees at Raleigh. Moore and Preyer restated their programs. Dr. Lake said that the next legislature would have to determine the financial condition of the state at that time before a general salary raise could be arrived at. He had said very little on the matter in the campaign as a whole. He had let Preyer fight the battle that was certain to be lost.

TAX REDUCTION

In Burlington, on February 5, Judge Moore proposed that families with small incomes be allowed to increase dependency exemptions on state income tax returns from $300 to $600.

The proposal was little noticed and was considered to be just campaign oratory. Few dreamed that Moore would be able to increase dependency exemptions for all North Carolinians during the 1967 General Assembly.

"SMOKING AND HEALTH"

On February 10, Judge Preyer followed Dr. Lake's lead in a speech at Albemarle. He noted that several states, in order to discourage the use of cigarettes, had proposed harsh taxes on them and said that the answer to the cigarette problem was research, not prohibition.

He later expanded this on March 4, at Windsor. There he said a strong effort should be made to obtain a federally financed tobacco research center in North Carolina.

Judge Moore mentioned the tobacco problem at Clinton on March 20. He said that the state should resist any "impetuous action on the part of the federal government which would damage our tobacco industry." However, he did not mention a research center.

On March 31, Dr. Lake told a Sanford audience that North Carolina should not wait for the federal government to provide a tobacco research center. He said that he would ask the legislature for the necessary money at the next session.

On April 17, Judge Moore told two hundred people in Dobson that the state should take the lead in promoting tobacco research and that the next governor should protect the tobacco industry from premature action by the federal government.

The same night, Dr. Lake, who apparently had advance notice of what Judge Moore would say at Dobson, told a Clinton audience that he was the first to come out for tobacco research, but that he noticed that the other two candidates had come out for the same thing.

Since all the candidates were then on record as favoring a tobacco research facility, nothing else was said about the matter during the first primary campaign. Apparently the candidates did not consider it important whether the facility would be financed by the state government or by the federal government.

THE RACE ISSUE

The race issue was the most important issue of the campaign. It was the issue that gave Judge Moore his overwhelming victory in the second primary. Yet there were many knowledgeable political people in the state who refused to admit that there was such an issue at all.

Democratic party chairman Bert L. Bennett, Jr., of Winston-Salem, was quoted as saying in the summer of 1963 that there should be no race issue in the next primary. He was concerned about party splits such as he had seen in the Frank Graham–Willis Smith senatorial campaign of 1952, and about the bitterness that he had seen result from the Sanford–Lake campaign of 1960. Once he was quoted by Charlotte reporter Joe Doster as saying that, of all issues Democrats could argue about, the race issue was the one "that don't put no meat on the table."

But the race issue could not be wished away. At the time that 16,000 people in Greensboro were signing a petition asking Judge Preyer to run for governor, during the last week of August, 200,000 Negroes and whites marched on Washington in the greatest civil rights demonstration in history. At the same time North Carolina newspapers were full of stories of Negro demonstrations in Williamston and other Tar Heel cities. On Friday of that week (August 30), Judge Moore announced that he would be a candidate. Politics and race could not have remained separated.

Moreover, the Negro "revolution" in America was the most important thing that was happening in 1963. The response of the people to that "revolution" was a matter that could not be entirely ignored.

Judge Moore recognized the race issue in his first major policy statement on October 12, 1963. He said, "The Negro deserves equality of opportunity, but it will not come through violence or civil rights legislation. I do not believe you can legislate equality. It must be earned." Newspapers were already speculating that Moore would emerge as the "middle-of-the-road" candidate between an arch-segregationist Lake and a liberal Preyer.

From the beginning, there were people in the Preyer camp who understood the importance of the race issue. Preyer was advised from one source that he should say no word which would indicate that he was friendly to the Negro cause. It was well known that Judge Preyer could not project himself as a conservative, but many hoped that he could be a true moderate and sell himself to the people of North Carolina as such. He was advised that the people of North Carolina in 1964 were not looking for a moderate-progressive or a moderate-liberal, but for a moderate-conservative. Preyer was advised to keep Negroes from participating in his campaign, even at the risk of offending some of their leaders. He was told that under no circumstances should he meet privately with Negro leaders; that if there were to be such meetings, they should be held in public with the press in attendance. The following statements were suggested for use at any such meeting: (1) that he could not encourage their demonstrations; (2) that he could not encourage any protest that involved the breaking of any law; (3) that there would be no reverse discrimination in North Carolina, if he became governor; (4) that integration of the public schools was not a cure-all for the state's race problems or cultural problems and should not be encouraged, although no federal court orders would be disobeyed; (5) that we must maintain the "fifth freedom," the freedom of the individual to choose one's associates. Other advisers went so far as to tell Judge Preyer that he should make a major anti-Negro speech.

Judge Preyer patiently received all of these suggestions and many others, but was more persuaded by the argument of another associate: "Rich, I don't believe that you could convince the people of North Carolina that you were anti-Negro if you publicly flogged one on Jefferson Square in Greensboro."

Judge Preyer reportedly replied, "And if I did flog one, Dr. Lake would be quick to point out that I didn't look like I enjoyed it very much."

Judge Preyer was not a segregationist. He could not make statements indicating that he was. Therefore he could not make an anti-Negro speech. He was opposed to the Civil Rights Bill. He felt that it was unconstitutional to force an owner of private property to serve persons that he did not desire to do business with. During the campaign he would repeat many times that he was opposed to the Civil Rights Bill, but the less liberal elements in the state seemed to sense that he was not opposed to the bill in quite the same way that they were.

Because of Judge Preyer's deep convictions, he could never satisfy all the requirements of the majority of North Carolinians, who were themselves segregationists. They could accept a Terry Sanford, who was born and reared a segregationist but who suppressed that side of his nature to preach good will among the races (although many of his supporters left him when he came out for fair employment practices in state government). Sanford was an Eastern North Carolinian and understood the mind of the people he had lived among. They sensed that he understood. In the same way, they sensed that Preyer was different.

On February 12, Judge Moore refused an invitation to meet with a group of Eastern North Carolina Negroes, the N.C. Joint Committee on Health and Citizenship. Joe Branch, Moore's state campaign manager,* charged that the invitation

* Later appointed by Governor Moore to the North Carolina Supreme Court.

was a frame-up. He said that Preyer's manager, Nat Townsend, had met with the Negro group two weeks previously at Washington, N.C., and that Preyer forces were concerned over the publicity which the incident received. He claimed that Preyer's men had then instigated an invitation to Moore. On February 15, Preyer issued a statement defending Townsend. He said that Branch had tried to make an open meeting appear "wrong and sinister," adding that he would not foster strife or discord between the races.

On February 19, Moore, speaking in Concord, accused Townsend of having invited all the Negroes attending the Washington meeting to dinner after the meeting and said that 128 had accepted.

A SANFORD-BENNETT MACHINE?

On February 17, Moore issued a statement from Statesville attacking what he called the "Sanford-Bennett Machine." He accused the Sanford administration of "brazen perversion" of public office and said that the Governor and his aides were using pressure and coercion, particularly among state employees, to insure the election of Preyer.

Sanford refused to comment.

CHAIN BANKS

On February 28, Dr. I. Beverly Lake, speaking before the Greensboro Civitan Club, charged that certain chain banks in the state were supporting his opponents with money and were "issuing directives to their employees instructing them how to vote." He went on to say that the "power of life and death" over industry and agriculture should not be concentrated in the hands of three or four bank chains. He tied this danger to the civil rights issue by saying that if the banks were under the domination of the Attorney General they might call the loans of motels and restaurants who refused to integrate their facilities. He said that "bank after bank has ceased to be an independent institution and has been swallowed by a larger bank with headquarters in another city."

THE UNITED FORCES FOR EDUCATION PROGRAM

L. Richardson Preyer issued a statement from Raleigh on February 28 endorsing the program of the United Forces for Education. The program included a 5 per cent pay raise for teachers each year for two years and a reduction of the classroom load. Preyer estimated that the cost of such a program would be $65.6 million. He said that, of the funds available, he intended to give education priority.*

On March 18, Judge Moore told a rally in Nashville that he supported the UFE program to the extent that "funds are available."

THE "SPEAKER BAN" LAW

On March 3, in a speech at Chapel Hill, Judge Moore said that the 1963 law which barred Communists from speaking on the campuses of state-supported colleges and universities was unnecessary. He said he did not think "we need the law."

---

* Endorsement of the program of the United Forces for Education first became important in the 1952 primary when Hubert Olive and William B. Umstead were running. Olive had worked long and hard to build key support among teachers, but when the UFE announced its program that year, it was Umstead who quickly seized it and promoted it across the state. Olive never regained the offensive on the education issue and was defeated.

In 1960, it was Terry Sanford who grabbed the UFE program and ran with it. He had learned his lesson well from the Olive campaign.

In the 1964 campaign, Lake never endorsed the UFE program. Preyer and Moore both endorsed it, but only to the extent of funds available without additional taxes. Sanford, of course, in 1960 had said that he would ask for new taxes to support the UFE.

On March 11, Dr. Lake told the Wake Forest YDC that he favored the speaker ban.

MOORE FORCES HAVE THEIR BIG RALLY

On March 6, five thousand people attended a Moore rally at Raleigh. One newspaper headlined, "Midst dancing and singing and elocuting, Moore files."

In his speech to the group, Moore promised to locate a qualified State Industrial Development Specialist in every congressional district in North Carolina. He said that the cost would be small in terms of the over-all budget.

FREE TEXTBOOKS?

On February 13, Judge Preyer said in a speech at Dunn that he favored elimination of all textbook fees.

On March 12, in High Point, Dr. Lake said that he would ask the legislature not only to give free textbooks, but also to give free classroom supplies, "such as paper, pencils, workbooks, and the like."

THE HIGHWAY BOND ISSUE

Judge Preyer restated his call for a new highway bond issue over and over again.

Dr. Lake attacked Preyer's proposal on February 18 in Goldsboro by saying that the state was not presently getting full value for the road-tax dollars spent. He said that $360 million had been spent on roads during the preceding two years, but that the state had not received $360 million worth of road building and maintenance. He did not specify what had happened to the "unaccounted-for funds," but implied that they had been squandered in inefficiency.

On March 12, in Shelby, Richardson Preyer put his road

program in terms that could be understood by the voters. He said that there were still more than 22,000 miles of unpaved roads in the state over which school buses had to travel. On March 26, Preyer was quick to endorse the program of President Johnson's Appalachian Regional Commission, which planned 139 miles of highways in the mountains of North Carolina. Moore said that he was for the President's program only if it could be administered by the state, rather than by the federal government.

On April 14, when Dr. Lake set forth certain conditions for his participation in a television debate, he specified five subjects that must be discussed: (1) the Speaker Ban Law, (2) the Civil Rights Bill, (3) education, (4) family income, and (5) taxing and spending policies. He did not view the road issue as of sufficient importance to include it on his "must" list. On April 21, in Durham, Dr. Lake accused Preyer of conflicting proposals on the road bond issue. He said that his opponent had first talked of a $200 million issue, later of a $300 million issue, and still later of a $350 million issue.

Dr. Lake continued to talk about the road program and continued to accuse the Sanford administration of not giving the people their money's worth for road funds spent. He continued to call for a "steadily proceeding" highway program and for an east-west superhighway.

In the final weeks before the first primary, Judge Moore took the position that, if elected, he would appoint a committee to study the proposal for a road bond issue. During a day of campaigning in Yadkin County he told small groups that he believed that, if Preyer went into the governorship and carried out the bond issue, he would build up the most powerful political machine ever seen in the state. He felt that the having of such a huge sum to spend would cause such a political machine to develop.

THE PEACE CORPS CONTROVERSY

On March 16, newspaper readers were struck by the similarity of two news releases that appeared in papers around the state.

The first was a release from Judge Dan K. Moore. At a rally in Trenton, Moore proposed a state organization modeled after the Peace Corps as a means of fighting illiteracy and poverty in North Carolina. The organization was to be called the North Carolina Corps and was to be made up of college students and recent graduates. Moore said that the organization would be financed by funds from foundations and other private donors and that workers would concentrate on problems of school dropouts, truancy, and other forms of delinquency.

The second release was from Raleigh and was an announcement by Governor Sanford of the formation of the North Carolina Volunteers, an organization of college students along the lines of the Peace Corps. Governor Sanford said that track star Jim Beatty has been selected to head the group. Volunteers were to be trained that summer and would work from September to the following August on a full-time basis. There were to be one hundred students who would work on ten comprehensive community projects sponsored by the North Carolina Fund. The Fund would defray the costs.

On March 17, Judge Dan K. Moore accused Governor Sanford of stealing his idea for a North Carolina group similar to the Peace Corps. Moore said, "I reject his claim to having originated such an idea. It is clear from published reports that Mr. Sanford's announcement was occasioned by my plan and judging from the marked resemblance his plan bears to mine he has borrowed liberally from a proposal we have been formulating ever since I entered the gubernatorial race."

In announcing the Governor's program the day before, a Sanford aide had said, "The Governor is announcing a program not a promise." Moore countered by saying, "I resent and reject his claim that the North Carolina Corps is a political promise while his theft is a program in being. It is painfully clear from Mr. Sanford's action in this matter that he has injected himself into the gubernatorial campaign in a direct attempt to discredit my candidacy."

At the Governor's office, John Ehle, a special assistant, gave this chronology of events leading up to the Sanford announcement:

July 6, 1963: A handwritten nine-page memo from Governor Sanford to John Ehle advancing the idea of a special corps and suggesting several names, including "Student Youth Corps."

October, 1963: Jim Beatty, track star, was approved as director of the corps.

November 2, 1963: The proposal was considered at a meeting of the Board of Directors of the North Carolina Fund, an agency created by Governor Sanford to handle foundation and public funds in his program to combat poverty in the state.

January 15, 1964: John Ehle approached the U.S. Office of Education in Washington to determine whether federal funds could be obtained for the project.

February 4, 1964: John Ehle called on the Peace Corps in Washington and talked about securing the services of former Peace Corps workers.

February 28, 1964: At a meeting of the North Carolina Fund Board of Directors, an appropriation for the project was approved.

March 11, 1964: The project was submitted to Washington to the U.S. Office of Education.

It should be stated from a historical standpoint that, although Sanford's plan was not announced until March 16, the record is clear as to the contacts with the North Carolina Fund, the U.S. Office of Education, and the Peace Corps prior to that date. The entire episode was the most unusual of the campaign.

THE GOVERNOR'S AIRPLANE

Judge Moore told a Dunn audience on March 19 that his first official act as governor would be to sell the governor's "expensive" airplane, the "Kitty Hawk," at public auction. He said that he thought economy should start in the governor's office.

On March 26, in Lumberton, Moore changed his mind. He said that he was not opposed to using the plane for industry hunting by the Department of Conservation and Development.*

ELIMINATION OF STATE JOBS

On March 20, Judge Preyer, speaking in Asheville, called for the elimination, in the interest of general economy in government, of state jobs that had been vacant for more than six months. On March 25, Dr. Lake criticized him for the statement, saying that the State Health Department had year-old vacancies for five public health directors, but that the salary ranges had not attracted qualified doctors to fill the positions. On March 31, Preyer told the Charlotte Optimist Club that he still thought the state should take a hard look at any position that went unfilled for six months. He softened his former position by saying that he would not immediately abolish such jobs but would require an explanation from the department head involved.

---

* The plane was in fact sold during the Moore administration, and a larger plane purchased.

CAMPAIGN HOME STRETCH

THE RACE ISSUE

ON APRIL 5, all three candidates appeared on the same platform at the same time and participated in a two-hour discussion sponsored by the Westminster Fellowship of North Carolina State College.

At this meeting, Preyer and Moore both agreed that, if the Civil Rights Bill became law, they would attempt to see that the law was enforced in North Carolina. Dr. Lake said that he would not "undertake to enforce" a law that he deemed unconstitutional. One questioner asked what the candidates would do about providing job opportunities for Negroes. Dr. Lake said that he proposed no program to promote jobs for a particular race. Moore said that he did not believe that we could legislate job opportunities. Preyer discussed a many-phased program for preparing persons for jobs and said that we should bear in mind that unemployment was three or four times higher among Negroes than among whites.

On the following Wednesday, April 8, Judge Moore took up the Civil Rights Bill again in a speech at Roanoke Rapids. He said that he was unequivocally opposed to the bill and that he did not believe "you can take from one citizen his constitutional rights and bestow them upon another."

The next day, Dr. Lake told a Raeford audience that professors convicted of violating laws in connection with racial demonstrations should not continue to teach at a North Carolina university.

During the same week the race issue took a new form as stickers saying "Negroes Welcome" were pasted on Preyer-for-Governor billboards in the Davidson County area.

On April 14, Dan K. Moore brought the race issue into the campaign in a new way. He charged that the Sanford administration (which he daily associated with Preyer) had put into positions of "state responsibility" persons who had encouraged racial demonstrations and who had advocated violations of the law. He named three young men who had been employed by the North Carolina Fund and the North Carolina Volunteers. George Esser, director of the North Carolina Fund in Durham, answered that the three named were not state employees, that he had hired them and not Governor Sanford or his administration, and that he would not employ anyone who advocated breaking the law.

On April 21, Dr. Lake embarked on his first major attempt to exploit the race issue. He began running full-page advertisements in several state papers on the Civil Rights Bill. In the ads he said that the bill was not moderate and had not been watered down but was the greatest "grasp for executive power conceived of in the 20th century." He called the bill the "Socialists' omnibus bill of 1963."

The next day, both Preyer and Moore felt that it was necessary to criticize publicly the racial demonstrations at the New York World's Fair.

On Saturday, April 25, at Rocky Mount, Judge Moore called the Civil Rights Bill a "constitutional mockery" and a "mixed bag of legalistic nonsense" and accused Richardson Preyer of saying that North Carolina needed to be concerned only with the public accommodations section of the bill. He continued his attack in a speech at Smithfield on May 4. Of the bill he said, "It will produce the greatest tyranny this country has known since the Revolutionary War." Of Preyer he said, "Could we dare put a liberal in the governor's office who is a captive of the NAACP and CORE?" (This was the first time that he had made this charge, but it would become the theme of his stop-Preyer efforts.) Nor did he allow Dr.

Lake to escape unscathed. He continued, "Could we dare put an extremist from the other side in the governor's office and chance the confusion of emotion with reason? Can we chance another Birmingham, or Little Rock, or Oxford, Mississippi, here in North Carolina?"

"Special Interests"

On January 27, 1964, Judge Moore had issued a statement saying that a much larger percentage of secondary road construction projects should be handled by private contractors. He said that, during the fifteen-month period ending December 31, 1962, 70 per cent of secondary road projects were completed by state forces.

This was taken by political observers to mean that Moore was either bidding for the support of the large road contractors or had it already and was issuing the statement to pacify them.

This short news release also foretold a part of the future of the campaign. Since the large road contractors had fought bitterly against Kerr Scott (at one time bringing a suit to enjoin the Highway Commission from building the new "Scott" roads with its own men and equipment), it seemed reasonable to assume that Moore would be appealing to the anti-Scott forces, or to the political heirs of those forces.

By the latter part of January it was a well-known fact that the First-Citizens Bank & Trust Company of Raleigh, headed by Lewis (Snow) Holding, was supporting Judge Moore. Moore buttons and leaflets were passed out over the counters in First-Citizens Banks in many cities. In Fayetteville, Cumberland County, Moore headquarters was installed in the First-Citizens Bank Building, and a Moore banner was draped across the front of the building. In several counties, First-Citizens Bank officers became campaign managers for Judge

Moore. In Raleigh, a First-Citizens Bank officer wrote a letter to all depositors of the bank urging them to support Moore. The letters were addressed on the bank addressograph plates containing account numbers. Many were struck by the novelty of receiving a letter about politics addressed "Mr. or Mrs. John Jones" or "John Smith, Custodian for Ray Smith."

Several persons who had borrowed large sums from First-Citizens complained privately that the way in which Holding solicited their support for Judge Moore gave them the feeling that he was putting pressure on them.

First-Citizens was not the only bank to become involved in the campaign, however. There were rumors to the effect that Carl McCraw, president of the First Union National Bank of Charlotte, was supporting Judge Preyer, as he had supported Governor Sanford in the preceding campaign. The Wachovia Bank and Trust Company and the North Carolina National Bank were not expected to support the man who was being promoted by Mr. Holding, and neither were they expected to support Dr. Lake. Therefore they were judged to be in the Preyer camp.*

But the other large banks were in a situation very different from that of First-Citizens. First-Citizens was completely controlled by the Holding family. The other banks had major stockholders who were widely scattered and who had varying interests. For example, First Union had over four hundred local directors located in forty-three cities in North Carolina. Some of these directors were Republicans, some conservative Democrats, some moderate Democrats, and some liberal Democrats. Therefore, there could be no official bank position on a candidate. There were major stockholders and directors

---

* It later developed that Wachovia's leading officers mostly supported Moore. North Carolina National was split between Preyer and Moore.

who supported each of the three candidates. No memos were sent from the home office to branches urging support of a candidate. During the last few days of the first primary, however, an executive vice-president of First Union was assigned to telephone other executives throughout the system who were known to be sympathetic to Preyer and get their aid in soliciting funds for the campaign. The other two major banks also had diverse ownership and divided directorates. Moreover, the top banks traditionally were worried about offending customers by taking a public role in a political campaign. Mr. Holding decided that these were secondary considerations as far as First-Citizens was concerned.

Nineteen sixty-four was not the first year that banks had taken a quietly active role in North Carolina politics. For many years, the Wachovia Bank and Trust Company had been very politically minded. In the days before Kerr Scott became Governor, millions of dollars in state funds were deposited in banks across North Carolina without interest. It was very important for a bank to be in touch with all political happenings. Wachovia employed as a trust officer a politically active former member of the General Assembly, Leroy Martin, and for many years thereafter he remained a familiar figure in the legislative halls and in the campaign headquarters of chosen gubernatorial candidates. During the Umstead–Olive campaign in 1952, insiders stated that Mr. Martin brought over $40,000 to the Umstead campaign chest. It was explained that this money was not donated by Wachovia, but was gathered from friends and customers of the bank. In 1960, political circles buzzed with rumors about how Wachovia first considered supporting Addison Hewlett of Wilmington for the governorship, then turned to John Larkins, and finally wound up supporting Malcolm Seawell. At the end of the first primary in 1960,

Wachovia turned to Sanford in preference to Lake, and, according to reliable sources, gathered more than $20,000 for the Sanford campaign chest. Through all of this, the Security National Bank of Greensboro (later to become part of the North Carolina National Bank) was courting all the candidates and making only very small contributions. At that time, First Union National was getting into state-wide politics for the first time and gathered some funds for Sanford.

On April 10, Judge Preyer called for a new lobbying law and said that Dan K. Moore was a candidate surrounded by lobbyists and special interests. He said that, of 127 lobbyists registered with the Secretary of State, only 85 listed any expenditures. He added that the other 42 merely stated that they were on annual retainers. Two days later Moore said that Preyer's statement was "false from beginning to end" and that he knew nothing which necessitated a new law on lobbying. He said that Preyer's manager was a member of a law firm that registered for lobbying purposes, that Preyer was backed by special financial interests, and furthermore that he was backed by the NAACP. The Raleigh *News and Observer* headlined Moore's statement with "Moore Backs Lobby Groups." This caused Moore to take an advertisement in the same newspaper the next day to refute the implications of the headline.

Preyer hammered at this theme again in Hickory on April 16. "Why shouldn't general counsels of large corporations . . . be required to register and report their expenses like other lobbyists?" he asked. He continued to include the proposed new lobby law in all his speeches and many of his advertisements throughout the remainder of the first primary campaign, but held his fire on "special interests."

During this period a number of Preyer's advisers, including

Major L. P. McLendon of Greensboro and Tom Pearsall of Rocky Mount, urged him to name the persons making up the "special interest" group around candidate Moore. At the time, however, Preyer correctly felt that he was the front runner and that Dr. Lake might run second. If this occurred, he would need the help of Moore in the runoff. Therefore he did not feel it wise to do anything spectacular which might backfire. The first primary passed without any more specifics on "special interests."

Minimum Wage

Early in the campaign Judge Preyer called for a new $1.00-per-hour minimum wage in North Carolina. Judge Moore then made statements which were generally interpreted to mean that he was opposed to any increase in the minimum wage.

On April 20, Moore contended in a speech to the Charlotte Kiwanis Club that he had never said "that the state minimum wage should not be raised under any circumstances." He said, however, that the legislature should be reasonably sure that the increase would not wipe out jobs instead of creating them. The *Greensboro Daily News* (which supported Preyer) headlined its report of Moore's speech, "Dan Moore Backtracks on Wages."

The same day, in Colerain, Preyer told a rally that increasing the minimum wage to $1.00 would help 55,000 working people.

The Rural Electric Cooperatives

On April 23, in High Point, Judge Moore was interviewed on a program called "Focus" at television station WGHP-TV. One reporter asked if Moore thought that REA's should be taxed as private power companies were taxed. Judge Moore said that he believed that when an REA was small and just getting started, it should not be taxed, but that after it was "operating in the black," it should pay taxes like any other corporation. This position, of course, was unacceptable to the supporters of the REA's.

Preyer, apparently feeling that he had no support left in the private power companies, made several speeches in which he criticized the Utilities Commission, and, by implication, the power companies, and said that, if it became necessary, he would go to the legislature and ask for reorganization of the commission.

On May 23, one week before the first primary, Judge Moore was touring Yadkin County. At a small gathering at a fire station, a man in the audience asked Moore about his position on the REA. Judge Moore said that he came from an area in the mountains that had been developed to a great extent by the REA's, and that he supported them.

The campaign for the first primary ended without Dr. Lake making any public pronouncement on the REA question.

PROBING FOR THE LAST VOTE

The latter part of April and most of May were consumed with statements by the candidates about things that never developed into major issues. For example, on April 29, Judge Moore gave out a press release favoring having prayer in public schools. He did not say whether he favored having governmental units prescribe the prayers, which was the issue in the Supreme Court case to which he alluded. On May 1, Moore proposed to revamp the Highway Commission again, saying that he would reduce the number of commissioners and restore the "point system" of road building which had been used in the Hodges administration.

On May 4, Preyer pledged progress in the field of mental health, and on May 6, Moore called for new emphasis on

North Carolina's livestock program, saying that additional food processing facilities should be established. On May 8, Lake added his criticism on the subject of the governor's airplane. He said that it cost $207,000 to purchase and $62,000 per year to operate, that it was an extravagance, and that he would get rid of it if he became governor. On the same day, Moore called for new emphasis on the first three grades in the public schools, echoing a proposal originally made by Lake on February 15.

On May 10, Preyer proposed new benefits to state workers, obviously trying to attract votes that seemed to be slipping away to Moore. He called for a new hospital insurance plan, additional longevity pay, and compensation for unused sick leave. He said the program would cost $2.5 million per year.

On May 11, Preyer called for a free school lunch program to reach 35,000 children who presently went without. The next day Moore told a Charlotte rally that, if elected, he would make certain that North Carolina schools taught patriotism. At the same hour, in Wadesboro, Preyer was telling farmers that he advocated personal involvement of the governor in the problems of agriculture.

On May 18, the silly season campaigning reached its peak. Judge Moore's campaign headquarters issued a press release saying, "Did Preyer know when he was 26 years old that he would be the handpicked candidate of Terry Sanford 19 years later?" "His name at birth according to the records was Lunsford Sanford Preyer," the release continued. It said that Preyer changed his name when he was twenty-six years old.

Investigation disclosed that the original birth certificate in Raleigh was correct, with the full name "Lunsford Richardson Preyer." The person who made the copy for Guilford County records transcribed "Sanford" for "Lunsford" and left out the middle name. Someone noticed the error and changed it about the time Preyer was released from the Navy, according to Nat Townsend, Preyer's campaign manager.

On May 25, Dr. Lake charged that one of his opponents had "become frantic" and was about to start using mud-slinging tactics. He did not identify the opponent, and no identifiable mud-slinging attack on Lake came.

THE RACE ISSUE

The key issue during the last six weeks of the campaign was, of course, the race issue. Preyer continued to mention that he was opposed to the Civil Rights Bill, but made no major speeches on the subject and ran no newspaper advertisements about his position. He did say that the Civil Rights Bill "interferes with North Carolina's way of solving racial problems." He also said that "law and order will be maintained in North Carolina" and that he would use the National Guard or any other force necessary to preserve law and order.

On May 14, Moore told a Wilmington audience that "violence or chaos by a minority, majority or Communists will be dealt with by rule of law, not by fuzzy-minded liberals who have confused civil rights with anarchy." He attacked the Attorney General for investigating police brutality in Nashville, but not investigating it in New York City.

On May 15, Preyer spoke to an integrated audience of 3,000 in Winston-Salem and plugged for "the North Carolina way" in race relations, a phrase that he would use over and over during the remainder of the campaign.

On May 20, the day of the State Democratic Convention, Judge Moore took identical advertisements in newspapers across the state to promote his position on the race issue.

"One candidate for Governor," said the advertisement, "doesn't seem to think the people of North Carolina have anything to fear from any part of the Civil Rights Bill except perhaps the one part that deals with 'Public Accommodations'." The ad continued, "Read why Dan K. Moore believes the people of North Carolina have a great deal to fear from EVERY part of this dangerous legislation."

The ad stated that, if the bill became law, the federal government could dictate to farmers who received federal funds whom they could hire and fire, and how much employees should be paid. It stated further that the federal government could dictate to those businessmen who would ultimately employ twenty-five people whom they could hire, fire, and promote, and how many whites they had to fire to employ more Negroes. One statement in the advertisement said, "Fighting to convict you could be Bobby Kennedy and the full power of the Federal Government."

The next day, May 21, Dr. Lake told newsmen in Dunn that he would take the lead in testing the constitutionality of the Civil Rights Bill if it were passed by Congress. He reaffirmed his belief that the bill was unconstitutional. However, it was noted by observers during Lake's Harnett County visit that he was saying less about the race issue than he had four years before.

On May 24, it was noted in state newspapers that anti-Preyer handbills were circulating in many counties. One leaflet entitled "Why You Should Vote for 'Rich' Preyer" listed as one of its "reasons" that "he is supported by such fine organizations as the NAACP, CORE, Martin Luther King, and James Farmer." The handbills were unsigned.

On May 27, in Kernersville, Dr. Lake again attacked the Civil Rights Bill and opponent Richardson Preyer. He said that Preyer was a federal judge and "ought to know that it is the federal government which enforces all federal statutes."

On Wednesday, May 27, the Preyer forces ran advertisements in local weekly newspapers in Eastern North Carolina stating Preyer's stand against the Civil Rights Bill.

On Thursday night, May 28, before the first primary, the Ku Klux Klan burned several crosses in the Wilmington area. The next day candidate Preyer took public note of the burnings when he landed in Wilmington on a one-day airplane tour of the state. He called for the "sane and sensible way" in race relations and said that the cross burners were "throwing kerosene on the fire and fanning the flames of race hatred." Dr. Lake's campaign manager, Allen Bailey, issued a statement the same day saying that the cross burnings were "silly and stupid."

The race issue reached its climax on the night of the first primary, May 30. Station WRAL-TV in Raleigh was the center of a state-wide television hookup for election night coverage. Partially owned by A. J. Fletcher, a former law partner of Dr. Lake, it was strongly anti-Preyer. Anticipating that the Negro vote in North Carolina would go to Preyer, the station prepared charts ahead of time showing predominantly Negro precincts in many areas of the state, leaving space for the vote figures. As the returns came in showing Preyer to be the overwhelming victor in these precincts, WRAL-TV presented its charts showing "Negro block-voting." These charts were presented time after time during most of the evening's election coverage. The effect was devastating. By the time the night was over the matter of race made front-runner Preyer the underdog. There was really no need for a second primary, but it was impossible for the man with the most votes to give up.

Of the votes cast on May 30, Preyer received 281,430, Moore received 257,872, and Lake received 217,172.

THE SECOND PRIMARY

THE MOORE FORCES were jubilant over the outcome of the voting. Dr. Lake declined to endorse another candidate immediately, but many of his supporters appeared at Moore headquarters on election night wearing Moore buttons. Although Preyer was front runner, there was only restrained celebrating in his camp. Two of the top workers in the Preyer camp knew how little they had to celebrate.

A week before the first primary, Phil Carlton, on the approval of Bert Bennett, Jr., had ordered a poll of North Carolina voters by an out-of-state firm (at a cost of $6,000). The poll had indicated that Preyer would lead in the first primary, but that 70 per cent of Lake's supporters would vote for Moore in the second primary. This was enough to give Moore a victory. Two other people knew the results of the poll: Governor Terry Sanford and Preyer himself.

On Sunday afternoon, May 31, Judge Preyer telephoned Dr. Lake asking for his support in the second primary and suggesting an appointment with him the following day. Lake was polite and noncommittal, but agreed to the appointment. On the same day Preyer challenged Moore to a series of television debates. Preyer said he thought the debates were so important that he was willing to accept any conditions within reason. He sent a telegram to the North Carolina Association of Broadcasters asking that they make time available. When asked for comment, Moore said that he would be glad to consider a TV debate if the time was made available.

On Monday, June 1, Moore issued a statement in which he flatly rejected the possibility of a debate. He said that his campaign plans did not include plans for a television debate. "I invite Mr. Preyer to tend to his own knitting," he added.

Lake and Preyer conferred on Monday, but reached no conclusion. Then Lake set up a series of conferences with his own supporters, which culminated in an announcement on Friday that he would support Moore. Insiders say that Lake gave serious consideration to Preyer's appeal. Preyer had avoided saying the harsh things about Lake that had characterized some of Moore's attacks. Some of Lake's supporters believed that Moore forces were responsible for the cross-burnings in the eastern part of the state on election eve. But Lake saw the mood of his people. As early as Tuesday, Lake headquarters at Dunn was converted to Moore headquarters without the authority of either candidate. In other sections, voters who had supported Lake warned their county managers, "Don't come back next week asking me to support that fellow Preyer."

The strategists for Preyer decided that they would try to force Moore into the needed television debate. A spot announcement was recorded for use on radio and television in which a country voice asked, "Where is the Mountain Man?" Many considered the ad to be in bad taste. Even Phil Carlton, whose voice was used, says that he opposed it. But Bert Bennett, the man with the final authority, insisted that the "Mountain Man" ad be broadcast, saying that Preyer's only chance to win was to "rock the boat." (Indeed, it should be said in Bennett's behalf, that he was right. Preyer had two choices: (1) to run a gentlemanly campaign to sure defeat in preparation for some future campaign, or (2) to "rock the boat.")

Many in the Preyer camp felt that Moore would have to debate whether he wanted to or not. They remembered that Terry Sanford had said that he would have lost to Dr. Lake if he had not accepted Lake's debate challenge. But Moore (and his strategists) felt that he had more to lose than to gain in such a debate.

The Preyer forces bought time on a television network for the night of Friday, June 12, and notified Moore that a chair would be provided for him in the studio if he decided to make an appearance. Moore did not choose to attend, and the telecast became known as the "Empty Chair Debate."

THE RACE ISSUE

On the Monday following the first primary, when Moore issued his statement rejecting the TV debate challenge, he also said that Preyer owed his lead and "the major part of his entire vote to the bloc of Negro votes in North Carolina" and that "this vote hangs like a millstone around his neck."

Preyer immediately accused Moore of injecting the race issue into the campaign and said that defeated candidate Lake had not done so in the first primary. Obviously Judge Preyer was taking a very narrow view of what constituted the race issue. It is hard to believe that he did not recognize the hard campaigning of his opponents against the Civil Rights Bill as the same old race issue that had plagued other North Carolina campaigners for years.

The same day Jesse Helms, vice-president of WRAL-TV in Raleigh, told Eastern North Carolina on his editorial program that, if it had not been for the Negro vote, Richardson Preyer would have received less votes than Moore or Lake.

Within a matter of hours former Lake workers in Eastern North Carolina were jumping on the Moore bandwagon and passing the word that "a vote for Preyer is a vote for the Nigger."

On June 4, a reporter asked Judge Moore whether or not he would continue the Good Neighbor Council which had been set up by Governor Sanford to work with race problems. Moore answered that he did not know enough about the council to say whether he would continue it or not.

On June 5, the day that Dr. Lake threw his support to

Moore, the latter denied that he had injected the race issue into the campaign, and Preyer said, "There is no real difference between Dan Moore and me on the race issue." In a further statement he said, "The only difference is that I'm not going to tear [the state] apart by . . . setting white against colored. The only thing a candidate can promise about dealing with the race issue is that he will deal with it fairly, honestly and firmly, without being controlled by extremists on either side—and with the help of God."

Moore immediately launched newspaper advertisements on education and began making speeches on unifying North Carolina, but the people of Eastern North Carolina were talking race.

The race issue was raging so hotly in Eastern North Carolina that in certain places it became somewhat a disgrace to have been associated with Preyer. In Harnett County, Harvey M. O'Quinn, who was engaged in a second primary race for county commissioner, ran an advertisement in the June 11 issue of the *Harnett County News* saying, "I was accused of working for Mr. Preyer the first primary. That was a mistake. I voted for Dr. Lake." Surely this will go down in history as the only time anyone ever admitted being for a losing candidate.

"SPECIAL INTERESTS"

On June 3, while Preyer was trying to "smoke out" Moore for a television debate, he got a little rougher. He said that "self-serving lobbyists are running and financing Dan Moore's campaign and are trying to hide that fact from the people of North Carolina." He added, "He has made his bed and we intend to see that he sleeps in it."

On June 8, at a meeting of businessmen at High Point's

String and Splinter Club, an aging Capus Waynick spoke with emotion about the matter of special interests. Waynick, who had managed Kerr Scott's campaign for governor, and who had later been ambassador to two Latin American countries and Adjutant General of the North Carolina National Guard, told of the days when the highway contractors and equipment dealers tried to dictate to Scott (no one could) and said that such a "coterie of special interests" was at that moment seeking to get control of the governorship.

Two days later, Preyer named the men who he said made up the "special interest" group around Moore.

Lewis (Snow) Holding was named because of his and his bank's activities in the campaign and because Preyer felt that Holding was in the campaign for more than just a general interest in good government. Holding replied that he had worked openly for Judge Moore and was proud of it. Edwin L. Jones, Jr., of Charlotte was named because he was the man who had written a letter to contractors across the state saying that Moore was pledged to "phase out" road work by state employees.

Dick Thompson of Raleigh was mentioned because he was an official of the North Carolina Equipment Company who worked full time for the Moore campaign.

Wade Barber of Pittsboro was specified because of his long record as a lobbyist for the Duke Power Company. Barber said that Preyer's statement was "ridiculous" and "without foundation."

Nello Teer, Jr., of Durham was named, not only because he was a large highway contractor who was supporting Moore, but because his company had been the plaintiff in an old lawsuit to stop Kerr Scott from building roads with state men and equipment. Teer had a sharp comeback. He said that Preyer had sought his support earlier in the campaign, and furthermore that the T. A. Loving Company of Goldsboro, another large highway contractor, was supporting Preyer. Preyer admitted that both allegations were true. He distinguished his case by saying that he did not seek Teer's support with "the promise Dan Moore has made to the contractors" and that his contractor supporters were helping him without promise.

He also named Armistead Maupin, Raleigh attorney, who had been a lobbyist for the small loan companies and the billboard industry. These were supposed to be examples of sinister "special interests" (although at that moment both Preyer and Moore were the greatest supporters of the billboard industry in the state).

C. V. Henkel of Statesville was named because of his lobbying efforts against the $1.00 minimum wage. Henkel issued a statement the next day saying that Preyer's attack showed his "complete ignorance of state government." He said that he had vigorously supported the North Carolina minimum wage law in 1959. He failed to say that this was an 85-cent wage rather than the higher figure that Preyer referred to.

Were the seven men named a "special interest" group?

In the broad sense that they represented corporations and business groups who might want favors from government to a greater extent than the average citizen, they were.

Was there anything secret about their activities? Generally speaking, there was not. Certainly all supported Mr. Moore openly. The money that they furnished to the campaign was not intended by them to be known to the public, but that was true also of Preyer's supporters. It is possible that Mr. Jones would have preferred that his letter to the contractors of the state remain "confidential," but it is unlikely that he really believed it could so remain. Mr. Holding's First-

Citizens Bank disbursed cash in small bills to Moore managers in Eastern North Carolina during the second primary for use in the precincts. While this was done in a secretive manner, Holding certainly knew that such transactions would be a topic of conversation between political buddies within a short time. After all, someone had to handle the cash, and a bank was the logical choice.

Was there any cohesive relationship between the seven men named? Certainly not. It is unlikely that they ever met as a group or acted together in any way. They were individuals supporting Judge Moore.

Were these seven men supporting Judge Moore for any reason other than an interest in good government? They said they were not, but the average voter must view their answer with some skepticism.

On June 10, when Preyer had accused Moore of being surrounded by "special interests," the latter replied, "We consider that Mr. Preyer, with his Vick Chemical empire, is a special interest himself." He referred to Preyer's family connection with the Richardson-Merrill Company, formerly the Vick Chemical Company. While this was a natural reply in the heat of politics, it is interesting to note that Judge Preyer had no voice in that company. As a young man he had once wanted to become a part of Vick. His father was president of the company and his maternal grandfather had founded the organization. But the company had learned that it could not attract bright young men if members of the family were to be employed on the same job levels. Therefore young "Rich" was ruled out and thus began a distinguished career as a lawyer and a judge.

On June 23, all seven of the men Preyer had named as Moore's "special interests" appeared on a program at Charlotte. Each began his talk with, "I am here because I have a special interest—a special interest in good government."

Throughout the remainder of the campaign Moore criticized Preyer for his "campaign of bitter abuse" and for "attacking persons supporting me." He said that he did not see any reason why the men named should have to endure such abuse.

The Rural Electric Cooperatives

Judge Moore became much more concerned about the REA matter during the second primary campaign. On June 10, at Smithfield, he made a strong statement in behalf of the co-operatives. He said that he would oppose any effort to weaken the REA's. In Kinston on the same day he declared that he would fight any attempt to put the cooperatives under the Utilities Commission. "I think every North Carolinian can take pride in both our rural cooperatives and our private power companies," he said.

On June 20, Judge Moore ran newspaper advertisements listing what he termed "false charges" of the opposition. He listed as a false charge that "Dan Moore would put the R.E.A. out of business." Then he listed his answer. "Dan Moore has stated, not just once, but on many occasions, that he would never be a party to the liquidation of our Rural Electric Co-operatives. He sees no need for placing them under the N.C. Utilities Commission. He recognizes their significant contribution to the growth of this state and would do nothing to impair the services they are providing. Dan Moore believes the REA's and the investor-owned power companies can continue to operate in harmony, providing electric service to their customers."

Since the phrase "investor-owned" is not ordinarily used by laymen in conversation or in writing, but is a key term used in all the advertising of the private power companies, one is tempted to speculate as to the authorship of that portion of the Moore advertisement. The same words were repeated in another (different) advertisement on the Thursday before the second primary.

TOBACCO

The second tobacco issue developed on May 27, but was not mentioned until the second week of the second primary. A group of tobacco growers in Georgia and Florida brought a suit in federal court against the U.S. Department of Agriculture and obtained a permanent injunction against placing a 10 per cent acreage cut into effect.

Preyer spoke on the matter on a state-wide television hook-up from Charlotte on June 12 (the so-called "empty chair debate" program). He said that he was outraged by the Georgia-Florida decision; that if the decision stood, the tobacco economy of North Carolina was threatened as never before. He said that he would sit on the desk of the Secretary of Agriculture, would do whatever was necessary to get the decision changed.

Preyer's statement came on Friday night. Over the weekend Governor Sanford announced that he would go to Washington on Monday to see Secretary of Agriculture Orville Freeman about the matter. Judge Moore called at the office of the Attorney General of North Carolina to determine the feasibility of the state intervening in the suit. Both Preyer and Moore issued statements.

On Monday, the U.S. 5th Circuit Court of Appeals suspended the lower court injunction until the merits of the case could be finally determined, and Governor Sanford did not go to Washington. But this did not end the matter. During the heat of the weekend Sanford had made a general statement to the effect that, if something wasn't done about the Georgia-Florida decision, North Carolina might have 10-cent tobacco again. On Tuesday, Senator Sam J. Ervin and Senator B. Everette Jordan issued a joint statement from Washington criticizing what they termed "demoralizing and loose talk about 10-cent tobacco." It was a curious statement, pointedly in criticism of Sanford. Curious because Sanford had always maintained outwardly cordial relations with the two senators, even though they differed. On one occasion Sanford had said that he liked the job that Jordan was doing in Washington and had no intention of running against him.

Even at this point, Sanford chose not to criticize Jordan, but he came back with a blistering attack on Ervin. He said that he had never indulged in criticism of Senator Ervin, but that he thought the latter should "quit criticizing me for fighting for the tobacco farmer and start helping." He said that he had been in on the fight for the tobacco farmer at every turn but that this was the first time he had seen Senator Ervin on the "fighting grounds."

On Wednesday, Moore said that the danger to tobacco prices was not immediate because the support price for 1964 had already been raised from 55 cents to 57 cents. Preyer replied that this showed how little Moore knew about tobacco, because the average price that the farmers received in 1963 had been 58.5 cents, and that a poor market would take money out of their pockets even with the help of government support. He also contended that the battle was not over because the case still had to be fought out on its merits.

Preyer plunged forward as a champion of the tobacco farmer. He discussed tobacco questions in most of his speeches, particularly in Eastern North Carolina, promised to set up a Tobacco Commission to help reduce the amount of tobacco held by Stabilization under loan, and ran numerous newspaper advertisements publicizing his stands on tobacco.

On June 22, Moore severely criticized Preyer's Tobacco Commission idea. He said that it was just such a commission that originated the Georgia-Florida lawsuit, and that such a commission would interfere with the work being done by Tobacco Associates, Inc., the marketing agency for the five-state flue-cured tobacco belt.

On June 23, Horace D. Godfrey, administrator of the Agriculture Stabilization and Conservation Service, made a statement to the press praising Governor Sanford for helping speed the federal court order on the Georgia-Florida case. The department had been held up in mailing allotment notifications to tobacco farmers because of the case. Sanford had telephoned Circuit Judge Griffin B. Bell. The appeals decision was then dated and filed, and the Secretary of Agriculture was notified by telegram. Godfrey said that, under normal procedures, action under the court ruling would not have been possible for another week.

Hardly had this word reached the public before Congressman Alton Lennon of Wilmington, a Moore supporter, visited another Department of Agriculture official. After this visit he announced that his host was "astounded" at Horace Godfrey's letter of praise to Sanford, and said that Sanford had really accomplished nothing. Sanford replied that he had not claimed that he had done anything but try to help, and that furthermore Lennon was the man that they had caught red-handed doing something-or-other in the Kerr Scott senate campaign.*

The Preyer forces ran advertisements containing endorsements from tobacco farmers. On June 24, Preyer appeared on

---

* During that campaign, Lennon, a young lawyer from Wilmington who had recently been appointed to the U.S. Senate by Governor Umstead, was opposed by former governor Kerr Scott. Terry Sanford, a young lawyer from Fayetteville, was Scott's campaign manager. Lennon lost his bid for the U.S. Senate, but in a later campaign won a seat in Congress.

television at Washington, N.C., with a special message to tobacco farmers.

This sustained effort by Preyer to reach the tobacco farmers brought some worry to the Moore camp. They ran advertisements on June 25 entitled "Dan Moore sets the record straight on three important issues." One of these issues was tobacco. The advertisement said, "The intensity and gravity of the present situation is unequalled in the history of the tobacco industry. I feel very strongly that never before has the need for positive leadership in a crisis been more obvious." The ad went on to say that, only a few weeks before, Preyer had told a group in Wilson that the only thing he knew about tobacco was that he had represented a client who had been hit in the head with a tobacco stick.

That last claim has its comical aspect when placed alongside a claim by the Preyer forces that was published at the same time: "On radio last week, you were asked about MH-30, and you answered by talking about "MI-30." For your information, Mr. Moore, MH-30 is a tobacco sucker control, and MI-30 is a Rexall mouthwash. Should the tobacco farmers of North Carolina vote for a man who doesn't know the difference between a tobacco sucker control and a Rexall mouthwash?"

During that last week of the second primary campaign, the third blow fell upon the tobacco industry of North Carolina: the Federal Trade Commission ruled that cigarettes would have to be labeled as harmful to health. On the day before the primary, the Preyer forces ran advertisements outlining their candidate's "fighting program" for tobacco. Preyer said that he would: (1) "fight to keep labels off cigarettes," (2) "fight that Georgia decision," (3) "fight to get rid of surpluses," (4) "fight for acreage increase, not another cut," and (5) "fight for a tobacco research facility."

The same day the Moore forces ran an advertisement entitled "Mr. Tobacco Farmer—Stay on Guard." Among other things the ad said, "Mr. Tobacco Farmer, *beware* of 11th hour tactics as the political clock is about to strike 12. As you know, Governor Sanford, with several administration First Lieu-tenants, in a *desperate* last ditch effort to save the Governor's hand-picked candidate, Judge Preyer, from a terrific *defeat* in the Primary Saturday, has *unfortunately* injected the tobacco issue into the campaign."

And thus the farmers of North Carolina saw re-enacted the old ritual of politicians pleading for their votes on the basis that each was more concerned about their problems than the other. In this case the show was made even more ludicrous by the "tobacco stick" and "mouthwash" stories.

THE HIGHWAY BOND ISSUE

After the first primary, the road bond issue was lost in the scramble for three weeks. Then, on June 21, the Preyer forces listed "a new Kerr Scott Road Bond Issue" as an important part of their program in two advertisements, one entitled "Preyer Cares About Eastern Carolina" and the other en-titled "Comparisons That Really Count."

On June 24, three days before the second primary, Preyer ran advertisements showing the picture of a school bus on a dirt road and saying, "Are You Tired? — of too many school buses in the mud, of too much dust on the front porch and on the clean clothes line? — of too many windows having to be kept closed all the hot summer long?" The ad went on to urge support for the "Kerr Scott Method" of road building.

All of this brought no response from Judge Moore. He did not mention the road bond question during the entire second primary. He apparently felt that the people were more interested in other matters, and he was right. The state was more in-terested in the Negro question than in roads.

THE RACE ISSUE

On June 20, Moore ran advertisements throughout the state listing what he termed "false charges" which had been made against him. He listed as a false charge the following: "That Dan Moore is using the race issue." He listed the following as being the truth about that charge: "On May 31, Dan Moore acknowledged his awareness of news stories concerning bloc-voting. He admitted that this bloc vote had given the candidate of the Sanford-Bennett political machine a decided edge and that this would certainly be an important factor in the second primary. Statements concerning the race issue have come from his opponent with increasing frequency in recent weeks."

On June 21, Preyer ran advertisements in Eastern North Carolina saying, "Preyer *Cares* about Eastern Carolina and understands its problems." A subhead in the ad said, "Preyer is against the Civil Rights Bill and for a calm approach to race relations." No one could deny that Judge Preyer cared about Eastern North Carolina, but it was doubtful that he under-stood—understood the mind of that section on the race problem.

On June 22, in Hickory, Judge Preyer said that North Carolina did not need the Civil Rights Bill or any other device that would interfere with solving problems on the local level. He said that he would seek a test of the constitutionality of the bill if it became law, but that he did not want to use such testing as an excuse for civil disobedience.

On that same day a former Lake county manager, Cooper Hamilton of Jacksonville, revealed to the press a letter that Moore had written to Negro leader John W. Winters of Raleigh soliciting his support. Hamilton said that such letters had gone to other Negro leaders in Charlotte, Winston-Salem, and Wilmington, and that all these leaders "are presently or have been leaders of the NAACP and CORE in North Carolina." Preyer managers in Eastern North Carolina promptly ran a reprint of the Winters letter in advertisements that said, "Don't let anybody fool you. Dan Moore has asked for the Negro vote!" Moore issued a statement admitting the letter but denying that he had sought the support of Negro organizations. It was explained that thousands of these letters had been typed on automatic typewriters, each an individual letter to a name and address from a list. Moore said that Negro names had not been purged from the lists.

On Wednesday night, June 24, three days before the second primary, Dr. Lake went on television in behalf of Judge Moore. Among many things that he stated in a scathing attack on Judge Preyer was the following in regard to the race issue: "But is it not strange that the great bulk of Judge Preyer's support in the first primary came from people who had marched and demonstrated for the Civil Rights Bill, who have longed for its adoption, who have praised its authors and who now rub their hands in glee (at this point Dr. Lake rubbed his hands together forcefully) at the thought of how you will suffer when the heavy hand of a cruel, wheeler-dealer administration in Washington presses down this crown of thorns upon your head?*

"Why do the white and negro [the little "n" was used when Dr. Lake's speech was later published by Moore forces] people who have written for, spoken for, marched for and demonstrated for the Civil Rights Bill now vote en masse for Judge Preyer who says it's a bad bill? Is it not that these people believe his opposition to their favorite bill is a mere academic, intellectual opposition, which they can persuade him to put

* Here Dr. Lake speaks as if the Civil Rights Bill were already law. It actually received the final approval of the House of Representatives on July 2.

aside now that the bill has been passed by Congress? Is it not that these friends of his believe Judge Preyer has honestly, sincerely placed his own faith in the false and evil social and political philosophy of Chief Justice Warren, Bobby Kennedy, and Martin Luther King?"

On Thursday before the second primary, three Negro civil rights leaders in the Piedmont area claimed that their support had been solicited by Judge Moore. One of them, Jesse Jackson of Greensboro, leader of the massive demonstrations at that city in 1963, said that Moore had sent him a telegram on April 6 asking him to serve on a college advisory committee. The other two, one a nominee for the state House of Representatives and one a city alderman in Winston-Salem, said that they had been approached by former Mayor Marshall Kurfees in behalf of Moore.

On the night before the second primary, Judge Preyer went on television with Governor Sanford, L. P. McLendon of Greensboro (who had just returned from serving as counsel for the Senate committee which was investigating Bobby Baker in Washington), and Tom Pearsall of Rocky Mount. Preyer mentioned the Civil Rights Bill and said that he intended to see that it was tested if it became law, but if segregationists were listening for some word of real sympathy for their cause they were disappointed.

Thus on this anticlimactic note the campaign ended, and on this unfortunate issue the outcome was decided. The final vote was: Moore, 480,431; Preyer, 293,863. Preyer carried only seven counties: Burke, Davie, Forsyth (Bennett's home county), Guilford (his own home county), Montgomery, Washington, and Wilkes.

PEOPLE IN THE CAMPAIGN

The Moore State Organization

Joe Branch—state manager
Joseph M. Hunt, Jr.
C. A. Dillon—finance chairman
Lewis R. Holding
Robert Holding
J. K. Sherron—young voters
Mrs. John D. Robinson—women voters
Tom S. Secrest—office manager
Bob Griffin
Dick Thompson—finance & liaison with county managers
Ed Woodhouse—liaison with county managers
Tim Valentine—Eastern manager
Woodrow Jones—Western manager
John Alexander—area manager
Dick Mauney—area manager
Ben Prince—area manager
Bill Johnson—press
Bill Scarborough—press
L. S. Chakales—press
L. D. Hyde—college coordinator
Richard Hughes—assistant college coordinator

The Preyer State Organization

N. A. Townsend—state manager
Bert L. Bennett, Jr.
Phil Carlton—Raleigh office manager
Charles Kivett—Greensboro office manager
Howard Holderness—finance chairman
Eli Evans—research
Mrs. Gordon Maddrey—women voters

Art Weiner—"Young Adult" voters
Charles Clay—press
Perry Young—press
Nancy Bryan—press
Bill Whitehead
Frank Merritt
Jim Connell
Charlie H. Smith—area manager
William D. Caffrey—area manager
Ray King—area manager
Roy G. Sowers—area manager
Bob Futrelle—area manager

THE LAKE STATE ORGANIZATION

Allen Bailey—state manager
Robert Morgan
Don Matthews—Eastern manager
Armand Swisher—Western manager
Dallas Gwynn—area manager
Quincy Nimocks, III—area manager
Red Simpson—area manager
John Burney—area manager
George Penny—press aide
Alex Brock—campaign treasurer
Mrs. Horton Doughton—Eastern "Ladies For Lake"
Mrs. Kemp Stagg—Western "Ladies For Lake"

COUNTY MANAGERS—*First Primary**

	PREYER	MOORE	LAKE
ALAMANCE	Herman McLean	Roger Ingram	
ALEXANDER	Kermit Sherill Sloan Payne Ray Chapman	Ray Lackey	
ALLEGHANY	Alton Thompson	Clete B. Choate	
ANSON	Fetzer Mills Robert E. Little	Robert Cagle	
ASHE	Robert Barr Wade E. Vannoy, Jr.	Tom Cockerham Fred N. Colvard	
AVERY	Ken Anderson	Robert L. Brooks Harold Winters	
BEAUFORT	Graham Elliott	Lloyd P. Sloan Bill Hodges William Studdert Sam T. Carter William Rumley, Jr. Edward N. Rodman Thomas S. Payne, Jr.	G. E. Jackson

* Many Lake managers became Moore managers or co-managers during the second primary.

	PREYER	MOORE	LAKE
BEAUFORT (*continued*)		J. E. Edwards	
		Abbott Morris	
		Cecil Cherry	
		Frank Bonner	
		William F. Taylor	
		George Parker	
		Ray Moore	
		Charlie Yates	
		Burgess Whitehead	Worth Hester
BERTIE	Charles Griffin		
BLADEN	Giles R. Clark		
	Dr. Julian Keith, Jr.		
BRUNSWICK	Kirby Sullivan	G. E. Henderson	
		Paul Dennis	
		Hubert H. Bellamy	
		Mrs. Foster Mintz	
		Mrs. Hampton McBryde	
BUNCOMBE	Richard B. Ford	Lamar Gudger	
		J. G. Stikeleather	
		Mrs. George Shuford	
BURKE	Dr. E. W. Phifer	W. Harold Mitchell	
		Sam Ervin, III	

COUNTY MANAGERS—*First Primary*

	PREYER	MOORE	LAKE
CABARRUS	A. W. Thomas, Jr.	James H. Wilkinson, Jr.	
		Carlos Baldwin	
CALDWELL	Ted West	C. Frank Kennerly	
CAMDEN	William Jones		
	Frank Williams		
CARTERET	Ralph Styron	Bud Dixon	
CASWELL	M. S. Angle	I. W. Fitch	
CATAWBA	William H. Chamblee	Young Smith	
		Stanley Corne	
CHATHAM	Sam Rees	Thomas K. Wrenn	
	Carl Yates	Edward S. Holes	
CHEROKEE	Leonard Lloyd	Bob White	
		H. A. Mattox	
		Frank Forsyth	
		Jack Dickey	
		Herman Edwards	
		E. H. Brumby	
		William C. Stalcup	
		Dr. Charles O. Vangorder	
		Herman Brauer	

	PREYER	MOORE	LAKE
CHEROKEE (*continued*)		Mrs. Lucy Laughter Sam Jones Ty Burnette	
CHOWAN	Tom Shepard		
CLAY	Fred Palmer	Neal Kitchin David Burch	
CLEVELAND	C. M. Peeler	Robert F. Morgan Roy Dedmon Paul Wilson	
COLUMBUS	Ed. L. Williamson	Frank McGougan	
CRAVEN	Walter C. Jones, Jr. David Henderson	L. John Moore George Ipock	
CUMBERLAND	Charles Rose, Jr.	Wilbur Clark James Devane C. E. Jones James R. Nance Maurice Fleishman	Quincy Nimocks, III Bill Monroe
CURRITUCK	T. Baxter Williams		
DARE	Linwood Cuthrell Archie Burrus	Carlisle Davis	
DAVIDSON	Robert L. Grubb	R. F. Vanlandingham	E. K. Carter

COUNTY MANAGERS—*First Primary*

	PREYER	MOORE	LAKE
DAVIDSON (*continued*)		E. W. Hooper	Bruce Myers
		Eric E. Morgan, Jr.	
		John B. Craven	
		George L. Hundley	
DAVIE	D. J. Mando	Dr. Clyde Young	
DUPLIN	Claude Hepler	Robert L. West	
		Mrs. Winifred Wells	
DURHAM	Travis Porter	J. B. Brame	
	George Miller	J. A. McLean	
EDGECOMBE	W. G. Clark, III	Joel K. Bourne	
		J. O. Bishop	
		Alex Biggs	
FORSYTH	E. G. (Red) Lackey	James R. Fain, Jr.	
FRANKLIN	Roger Mitchell	Wallace Tippett	
GASTON	Dwight Beam	James Smith	
GATES	Allen E. Askew	F. R. Rountree	J. Darius Hill
GRAHAM	Leonard Lloyd	Ross Smith	
		E. W. Hooper, Jr.	
		Lloyd Millsaps	

County	PREYER	MOORE	LAKE
GRANVILLE	Steven Royster Sam W. Daniel	Wills Hancock Tom Allen	William T. Watkins
GREENE	Clifton Barfield	Robert S. Nimmo W. R. Price Jesse Thomas Hardy, Jr. A. C. Edwards	
GUILFORD	Arthur Kirkman Arthur O. Cooke	H. E. Seymour Arthur G. Corpening J. Archie Myatt, Jr.	Thomas E. Brown Mrs. Anne Martin
HALIFAX	Robert Carey Josey		
HARNETT	Robert Bryan Johnny Wilbourne Mrs. James Murray	Red Williams	Staley A. Spence
HAYWOOD	Pat Whitmire Bernard Crowell, Jr.	Dr. J. L. Reeves J. H. Woody	
HENDERSON		A. V. Edwards	
HERTFORD	Bynum Brown	Joseph R. Bryant Richard T. Vann	
HOKE	J. Bion Brewer Alfred Leach	Ralph W. Barnhart	
HYDE	Arthur Bell Harris		

COUNTY MANAGERS—*First Primary*

	PREYER	MOORE	LAKE
IREDELL	J. W. Johnston, Jr.	James M. Fraley	Tom Dillard, Jr.
JACKSON	L. H. Higdon		Harry Canaday
JOHNSTON	J. C. Woodard	Adam J. Whitley	
JONES	Bruce Johnson	Donald P. Brock	
LEE	Robert J. Bowers	Vernon Stevens	
	James E. Heins	Clawson L. Williams	
LENOIR	Paul Laroque	W. Harvey Turner	P. C. Barwick, Jr.
		Olin Reed	W. W. Kennedy
		Lloyd Whitfield	
		Alex B. Howard	
		Willie L. Measley	
		Elmer Wooten	
		Graham W. Turner	
		Clarence L. Stroud	
		R. A. Whitaker	
LINCOLN	James W. Warren	Perry Reep	
McDOWELL	Ernie House	S. J. Westmoreland	
		S. W. Blanton	
MACON	Bob Sloan	Woodrow Reaves	
		Richard Jones, II	

	PREYER	MOORE	LAKE
MACON (*continued*)		Jerry Suttan	
		Bob Siler	
		E. J. Whitmire	
MADISON	Liston Ramsey		
MARTIN	J. Paul Simpson		
MECKLENBURG	Joseph Grier, Jr.	Dr. L. Sidney Christian	
		Jake Wade, Jr.	
		Roy McKnight	
		Guy Carswell	
		James O. Cobb	
		George Broadrick	
MITCHELL	Lat Westall	R. B. Phillips	
MONTGOMERY	J. F. Allen	Leighton Brown	
MOORE	M. G. Boyette	Herman Grimm	
NASH	J. N. Sills	Roy A. Cooper, Jr.	
NEW HANOVER	Howard Penton, Jr.	Louis Poisson	
		Mrs. Hugh W. Primrose	
NORTHAMPTON	T. G. Joyner	R. L. Grant	
ONSLOW	Dan Southerland	Jim Strickland	
		Marion Godwin	
		John V. Huff	

COUNTY MANAGERS—*First Primary*

	PREYER	MOORE	LAKE
ORANGE	Dr. Kemp Jones Robert Satterfield	R. B. Fitch A. H. Graham Fred Cates	
PAMLICO	M. D. (Buck) Jones	George W. Smith Ned Delamar Wilson A. Brinson M. Dewitt Brinson Hal Rowe	
PASQUOTANK	Walton Jennette	C. Buxton Small	
PENDER	Reuben L. Moore	John E. Russ Mrs. Roland Howard	
PERQUIMANS	W. L. Ainsley Howard Pitt	Julian White Charlie Umphlett	
PERSON	James E. Winslow		W. R. Cates
PITT	Tom Andrews	James Cheatham, III Robert L. Ramey	
POLK	Robert Adams	Fred Smith	
RANDOLPH	Adam Beck	Paul Bell Marion Burke Allen Scott Mayor Troy Smith	Sam W. Miller Alton F. Culver

County	PREYER	MOORE	LAKE
RICHMOND	Raymond Goodman Elsie Webb Fred Bynum, Jr.	John T. Page, Jr.	
ROBESON	John Gardner	Ben S. Floyd, Jr.	
ROCKINGHAM	Dalton McMichael J. B. Balsley William Ivie	Thomas S. Harrington T. Clarence Stone	
ROWAN	Stahle Linn, Jr. Fred Corriher, Jr.	Rex E. Wood Clyde Harriss	
RUTHERFORD	Morgan Cooper	Woodrow Jones	
SAMPSON	K. E. Austin	Jack C. Morisey	
SCOTLAND	Wade S. Dunbar James A. Gibson	John F. McNair, III	John W. Flannery
STANLY	Bill Huckabee		
STOKES	Carlos Davis	William F. Marshall, Sr.	
SURRY	Carroll Gardner	Charles H. Randleman Roger Harris	
SWAIN	Leonard Lloyd	Odell Shuler T. D. Bryson, Jr.	
TRANSYLVANIA	Don N. Irwin	Ralph Ramsey Jack Potts	Joel Hubbard

COUNTY MANAGERS—*First Primary*

	PREYER	MOORE	LAKE
			Wiley Armstrong
TYRRELL	Larry Jones Waverly Phelps	Orville Howett	
UNION	Henry Smith	J. Max Thomas	
VANCE	J. W. Jenkins, Jr. D. Gray Faulkner	A. W. Gholson E. O. Faulkner	
WAKE	James Ray	Victor Bell Mrs. G. B. Cooper Richard T. Mauney John Alexander	
WARREN	Shelby Benton	Charles M. White, III James Y. Kerr	
WASHINGTON	Warnie Gurkin		
WATAUGA	Fred Mast		
WAYNE	W. Powell Bland	James N. Smith	
WILKES	Watson Brame	T. C. Goodman	
WILSON	John Webb	Roy Holford, Jr. Miss Naomi Morris	
YADKIN	Wade Hobson	H. B. Shore	
YANCEY	Mark Bennett	Lowe Thomas	

section ten

THE VOTE

VOTES CAST FOR GOVERNOR

COUNTY	First Primary May 30, 1964			Second Primary June 27, 1964	
	LAKE	PREYER	MOORE	MOORE	PREYER
Alamance	6,127	5,168	3,825	10,228	5,792
Alexander	226	611	1,347	1,834	690
Alleghany	241	987	1,148	1,428	861
Anson	1,273	1,372	1,221	2,714	1,674
Ashe	95	1,663	1,331	1,624	1,575
Avery	23	503	574	713	512
Beaufort	2,742	1,686	1,868	4,578	1,929
Bertie	1,288	927	507	1,912	1,096
Bladen	2,668	1,814	903	3,643	1,806
Brunswick	2,333	1,823	945	2,626	2,215
Buncombe	1,212	6,233	18,850	21,051	6,197
Burke	524	4,916	3,856	4,868	5,108
Cabarrus	1,839	3,162	4,058	6,013	3,150
Caldwell	429	2,676	2,848	3,335	2,720
Camden	508	291	321	735	328
Carteret	1,082	2,516	2,186	3,257	2,633
Caswell	1,366	794	991	2,348	874
Catawba	957	2,455	4,916	6,728	3,054
Chatham	2,094	1,844	1,555	3,913	1,816
Cherokee	39	110	2,544	3,141	190
Chowan	798	644	221	800	755
Clay	15	101	574	880	127
Cleveland	3,948	4,509	5,741	8,416	5,118
Columbus	4,958	3,441	3,138	6,534	2,891
Craven	2,788	3,412	3,010	5,459	3,340
Cumberland	6,312	6,553	2,385	9,250	6,418
Currituck	756	525	515	1,060	448
Dare	472	636	804	1,062	593
Davidson	1,878	4,224	4,735	7,090	4,583
Davie	296	941	577	1,056	1,100

	First Primary May 30, 1964			Second Primary June 27, 1964	
COUNTY	LAKE	PREYER	MOORE	MOORE	PREYER
Duplin	3,569	2,681	1,643	5,255	2,998
Durham	10,940	10,657	4,171	14,101	10,861
Edgecombe	2,932	2,403	1,863	4,850	2,392
Forsyth	4,235	14,593	8,704	14,620	15,655
Franklin	3,865	1,423	1,177	4,896	1,407
Gaston	3,058	5,284	5,657	9,467	6,054
Gates	505	341	550	1,090	413
Graham	9	689	652	720	638
Granville	3,028	1,561	1,253	4,256	1,469
Greene	1,766	690	868	2,302	872
Guilford	5,362	23,418	6,708	13,608	24,211
Halifax	4,947	3,682	3,852	7,514	3,641
Harnett	5,664	2,145	1,583	7,031	2,206
Haywood	539	1,802	6,764	7,977	1,921
Henderson	244	894	2,903	3,747	1,018
Hertford	1,527	1,792	933	2,041	1,554
Hoke	847	1,131	566	1,470	1,013
Hyde	452	463	442	840	474
Iredell	1,790	3,591	4,421	6,822	3,918
Jackson	114	479	4,391	4,389	434
Johnston	6,450	3,034	3,682	8,354	3,284
Jones	815	1,025	894	1,689	990
Lee	2,051	1,808	1,394	3,388	1,906
Lenoir	3,496	2,678	3,156	6,558	2,752
Lincoln	611	2,380	2,720	3,573	2,704
Macon	59	689	2,674	2,923	664
Madison	65	2,606	2,765	2,367	401
Martin	2,849	1,213	969	3,718	1,392
McDowell	376	1,429	3,685	3,872	1,326
Mecklenburg	7,688	18,178	13,987	23,153	18,712
Mitchell	29	300	697	898	335
Montgomery	575	1,481	940	1,671	1,833

County	First Primary May 30, 1964			Second Primary June 27, 1964	
	Lake	Preyer	Moore	Moore	Preyer
Moore	1,639	2,380	1,706	3,425	2,369
Nash	5,676	2,299	2,710	7,537	2,468
New Hanover	6,358	5,399	2,709	9,597	5,629
Northampton	2,115	2,331	1,079	2,973	2,339
Onslow	3,109	2,640	2,412	4,833	2,520
Orange	3,127	4,617	2,079	5,283	4,542
Pamlico	466	680	925	1,180	677
Pasquotank	2,122	1,851	496	2,147	1,934
Pender	1,746	1,628	837	2,564	1,737
Perquimans	813	559	329	908	580
Person	2,274	1,621	1,583	3,733	1,641
Pitt	4,363	4,099	3,563	7,596	4,480
Polk	166	399	1,912	1,842	347
Randolph	1,568	2,613	1,852	3,938	2,504
Richmond	2,662	3,387	1,669	4,964	4,026
Robeson	3,365	4,750	4,047	8,057	5,438
Rockingham	2,821	4,182	3,129	6,797	4,654
Rowan	2,625	4,291	4,176	7,746	4,765
Rutherford	1,169	2,764	5,041	6,333	3,253
Sampson	2,060	2,476	1,494	3,388	2,673
Scotland	1,434	1,634	1,169	2,452	1,462
Stanly	1,024	2,433	1,842	3,201	2,696
Stokes	695	1,426	1,705	2,816	1,745
Surry	635	3,305	3,590	4,889	3,483
Swain	47	480	1,612	1,704	516
Transylvania	275	1,044	2,964	2,966	1,057
Tyrrell	381	534	427	648	615
Union	1,625	2,290	2,481	4,017	2,150
Vance	3,768	2,422	2,065	5,314	2,385
Wake	15,104	13,378	10,005	25,127	14,443
Warren	2,716	1,731	579	3,066	1,589
Washington	1,276	1,239	472	1,192	1,484

| | First Primary
May 30, 1964 | | | Second Primary
June 27, 1964 | |
COUNTY	LAKE	PREYER	MOORE	MOORE	PREYER
Watauga	86	1,020	1,142	1,479	921
Wayne	4,243	2,865	2,845	6,738	3,301
Wilkes	349	3,271	1,471	2,864	3,680
Wilson	3,280	2,677	2,995	5,904	3,103
Yadkin	223	757	1,066	1,612	950
Yancey	23	881	1,536	2,145	666
	217,172	281,430	257,872	480,431	293,863

Other Democratic votes cast
in First Primary:

	Brewer	8,026
	Burleson	2,445
	Stansbury	2,145